Preventing Youth Suicide

Preventing Youth Suicide

A Handbook for Educators And Human Service Professionals

Marcia L. McEvoy, Ph.D.
and
Alan W. McEvoy, Ph.D.

LP **LEARNING PUBLICATIONS, INC.**
Holmes Beach, Florida

ISBN 1-55691-056-8

Learning Publications, Inc.
5351 Gulf Drive
P.O. Box 1338
Holmes Beach, FL 34218-1338

Printing: 5 4 3 2 1   Year: 8 7 6 5 4

Printed in the United States of America.

Cover design by Alan W. McEvoy

Dedicated to the memory of our father,
Harry K. McEvoy, 1910 - 1993.
Dad, you gave more than you took;
your spirit lives in that which you
created and in the love you left behind.

CONTENTS

About the Authors

Marcia L. McEvoy, Ph.D., is a school psychologist and prevention specialist at Allegan County Community Mental Health in Allegan, Michigan. She has helped to develop a comprehensive county-wide adolescent suicide prevention program in the schools, and has worked to implement and evaluate an exemplary peer assistance program which has received national recognition. She is a frequent speaker at national conferences, and has published articles on psychological testing, suicide prevention, and peer helping programs.

Alan W. McEvoy, Ph.D., is a Professor of Sociology at Wittenberg University in Springfield, Ohio. He has published extensively on the topic of intimate violence, including books on child abuse, on sexual assault, and on the exploitation of young people by family and peers. In addition to his many appearances on national television, he also serves as editor of the School Intervention Report and is a co-founder of the Safe Schools Coalition, Inc.

Acknowledgments

We are deeply indebted to our friends and colleagues for their encouragement and their constructive suggestions throughout the preparation of this book, especially Sally Beyer, Joanne VandenBerg, and Robert Welker. We are also indebted to the many students who served as a critical audience, patiently listening as ideas for this book were articulated and clarified.

Special thanks to our editor, Edsel Erickson, whose painstaking reading of drafts and intelligent analysis were basic to the success of this effort. Thanks also to Vicki DiOrazio for her skill and efficiency in setting the text. We are also grateful for the financial and other assistance we received from Allegan County Community Mental Health Services, and from Wittenberg University.

Finally, we thank our respective spouses — Terry Madden and Cindy Farley — for their love and tolerance, and our children — Kara, Maggie, Katy and Kyle — for helping us to keep in focus that which is central.

1
YOUTH SUICIDE
IN CONTEXT

During the past two decades we have witnessed a dramatic increase in the rate of youth suicide. No one is certain why. Dysfunctional families, physical and psychological exploitation, rampant substance abuse, alienation, improper socialization, escalating youth violence, community disorganization and many other conditions are cited as causes. Whatever the reasons, one thing is clear: our schools are in an ideal position to help.

This belief is more than an act of faith on our part. The recent proliferation of literature on youth suicide suggests others share our view that schools can make a positive difference in preventing it. We are encouraged by the innovative responses of many schools, and we are heartened that educators, human service professionals, legislators and others are being sensitized to the needs of troubled youth.

Yet this increased sensitivity is only a first step. Practical help is needed. Unfortunately, much of the scholarly research literature on youth suicide does little to guide the actions of educators and human service workers who are the "front line troops" confronting the problem. The seemingly pedantic concerns about fine theoretical or methodological points — although understandably important to the advancement of knowledge — seldom communicate practical information to those who can help our young.

Of even less value are the sensationalistic media accounts which demand that action be taken — or which implicitly blame schools and agencies for failure to take action — without considering the limited resources available to them. Such media hype is counterproductive to the extent that it unnecessarily raises fears and causes actions to be taken without proper planning.

Our goal is to provide an up-to-date and comprehensive resource which offers educators and human service professionals practical guidance in addressing the problem of youth suicide. This is not a book on theories of youth suicide, nor is its primary intent to direct scholars conducting research. Rather, we aim to help those who work directly with students.

This book draws upon basic knowledge, research, common sense, and the practical experiences of educators and other professionals who must confront suicidal students. Because the problems facing many students are so acute, there is a compelling need for sensible, down-to-earth guidance. This book offers educators and others the step-by-step help they need to build effective programs which prevent youth suicide.

Magnitude of the Problem

The suicide rate among young people in the United States and Canada has nearly tripled since the 1950s, with the largest increase occurring among those between 15-to-19 years of age (Davis & Sandoval, 1991; Garrison, Lewinsohn, Martsteller, Langhinrichsen, & Lann, 1991; Lester, 1991; Poland, 1989; U.S. Department of Health and Human Services, 1989). Next to accidents, suicide ranks as the second leading cause of death among teenagers and young adults. Furthermore, while there is debate on the true number of suicide attempts among young people, a review of current research suggests that approximately one-in-ten school-age adolescents in the United States have made at least one prior attempt (Kalafat & Elias, 1991). For every completed suicide, estimates range from between 50-to-200 attempts of varying degrees of lethality (Orbach & Bar-Joseph, 1993). This translates into over 6000 confirmed suicide deaths and approximately a half million attempts at self-destruction each year.

In addition to those young people who kill themselves or who attempt to do so, there are many more whose pain compels them to think seriously about suicide. There is growing evidence that for teenagers, thoughts of suicide, as well as suicide attempts, tend to increase with age and peak during high school (Vega, Gil, Warheit, Apospori, & Zimmerman, 1993). Although adults often are shocked at the prospect of young people contemplating or attempting suicide, many teenagers do not appear surprised at the problem.

Recently the Gallop Organization conducted a comprehensive national survey in the United States soliciting the opinions of teenagers (ages 13-to-19) concerning suicide. The survey found that 60% of the respondents knew another teenager who either attempted suicide and failed (45%), or who succeeded (15%) in taking his or her own life. In over a third of these cases, the person attempting suicide was a close friend or a relative. Furthermore, 62% of those surveyed believed that some or most teenagers had thoughts of committing suicide. Equally disturbing, 15% of the persons sampled reported that they had come close to committing suicide, and 6% reported that they had attempted suicide.

Not surprisingly, the rise in youth suicide has generated deep concern among mental health professionals, educators, medical professionals, parents and others. The problem also has stimulated considerable media attention. This in turn has provoked debate, criticism, fear, and calls for action on a variety of fronts. While no one can say with certitude why adolescent suicide rates are increasing, the finger of blame is pointed in many directions.

To confound matters, the literature often is vague and inconsistent regarding how to help our youth in crisis, or about how to prevent the conditions which set the stage for some young people to seek escape through self-destruction. There still is much to be learned.

Yet we do know that if communities are to stem the tide of adolescent suicide, prevention is essential. Unfortunately, many schools and agencies have not developed comprehensive policies to guide them in suicide prevention and intervention programming. Many have yet to develop guidelines to follow in the aftermath of one or more suicides. Effective collaboration between schools and human service organizations is still a problem, often because of poor communication and turf issues. Inservice training for educators who face students in crisis is limited or altogether absent in many districts. Worse, many people fail to admit that even the potential for teenage suicide is a problem in their community.

Nevertheless, there is reason for optimism. Suicide crisis hotlines exist in most large and medium size cities. In addition, a handful of states such as California, Florida, New Jersey, Texas, Wisconsin, and Virginia have mandated some suicide prevention programming in the schools. Other states such as Michigan are developing comprehensive health education programming which promises to reduce the risks many students face. Training programs for teachers and other school personnel in how to recognize and help students in need — though still in the early stages — are emerging in schools throughout the United States and Canada. Many community mental health organizations are beginning to collaborate with schools in developing suicide prevention and intervention programs. And peer assistance programs — programs many believe to be helpful — are emerging in schools and communities nationally.

It is also encouraging that our understanding of suicide no longer is viewed in isolation from other social problems. Youth suicide is linked to child abuse, sexual exploitation, substance abuse, running away, family turmoil, and a range of other ills. Furthermore, theories of youth suicide are moving away from oversimplistic psychopathological assumptions as a cause, to the examination of more complex interactions between the family and the environment. Equally important, a range of treatments are emerging which show promise in helping those in crisis. Included here are the services of not only mental health professionals, but also self-help groups.

There also is a vast network of service agencies providing help to troubled youth and their families in nearly every district in the nation. There are many national organizations in the United States and Canada which serve as key resources. Included here are organizations such as the American Association of Suicidology, Youth Suicide National Center, National Institute of Mental Health, Canadian Mental Health Association, National Committee for Prevention of Child Abuse, Centers for Disease Control, and others too numerous to mention. In other words, when compared to just a few years ago, there has been considerable improvement in our knowledge of the problem and in our ability to respond.

Although there is progress on many fronts, youth suicide has not ceased. In fact, many experts argue that the social conditions which place our youth at risk are more prevalent today than before. In addition, well-intentioned attempts to intervene in crisis situations oftentimes generate new problems. For example, mental health organizations come under fire for mishandling cases, for not responding to a crisis in a timely and effective manner, and for poor cooperation with schools and other organizations. Schools are also under fire for failing to recognize and refer troubled youth who need professional help. Some argue that "crisis management" rather than primary prevention dominates school and agency responses to the risk of student suicide. To the extent that more effort is given to containing problems rather than to preventing them in the first place, the critics are right.

Whatever the merits of these criticisms, three generalizations may be made with respect to our success in preventing youth suicide. First, it is at the school building level that prevention and intervention efforts will meet with triumph or failure. Second, the success of any community program to remedy the problem is contingent upon the willingness of school personnel, health professionals, human service workers, parents and others to cooperate with one another. Finally, any comprehensive approach to the prevention of adolescent suicide must involve the schools in more ways than simply referring troubled students to mental health agencies.

INVOLVING SCHOOLS

Teachers, counselors, administrators and other school staff are perhaps in the best position to observe and to help young people. Often they are the only adults who make a positive contribution when a student is in trouble. Because they care about our young, and because they know that self-destructive behaviors undermine learning, educators have a strong interest in reducing the conditions producing suicide. Unfortunately, however, our schools have not been as effective as they could be in alleviating the problem.

Reasons for Limited School Involvement

Despite the importance of involving schools in suicide prevention, educators generally suffer from a paucity of training regarding what they should and should not do. Many teachers, administrators and support staff are uninformed about procedures for identifying, referring, and following up on those students experiencing a suicidal crisis. Most teacher education programs do little more than make passing reference to the problem. It is also true that inservice training in this area is inadequate or altogether absent in many school systems. All too often the training "method" is "baptism by fire," where teachers and staff are thrown into crisis situations for which they are ill-prepared. Even when inservice training on youth suicide occurs, it is seldom more than an *ad hoc,* one-shot approach. Comprehensive and practical information for teachers, school counselors, administrators and others in contact with potentially suicidal students is critical. But useful information has been slow to develop and be disseminated to those educators in a position to help.

To illustrate, consider one of the conditions directly related to the problem of youth suicide — child abuse. Evidence suggests that it was not until the 1960's that violence toward children was "discovered" as a significant and widespread social problem. Prior to that time, child abuse commanded so little attention that even physicians encountering severely battered children failed to recognize the injury as abuse. In addition, it was not until the late 1970's and early 1980's that sexual exploitation of children and adolescents was given much attention. Even more recently, researchers have begun to explore the character of psychological maltreatment — both in the home and in the context of one's community — which is at the core of all forms of abuse (Garbarino, Dubrow, Kostelny, & Pardo, 1992; Garbarino, Guttmann, & Seely, 1986). Yet we know that physical, sexual, and psychological abuse are strongly linked to suicidal tendencies among many victims.

Another illustration comes from the research on substance abuse in families. Only recently has the term "children of alcoholics" (or COAs) been popularized. It was not until 1983 that the National Association for Children of Alcoholics was founded. Yet we know that children from substance abusing homes face many problems which are linked to suicide.

An understanding of all the conditions creating problems for our young is still emerging; educators can hardly be blamed for failing in the past to attend to the manifold complexities associated with youth suicide.

As knowledge increases, however, so too do the expectations for school involvement. Yet positively involving schools in addressing the problem is easier said than done. For example, we know that a disproportionate number of suicidal students come from seriously dysfunctional homes. However, there is a simple reason why this knowledge does not always result in educators taking timely action to help. There is the commonly held view that educators should not interfere with the authority of parents in matters of child-rearing. As such, many are understandably reluctant to address student problems stemming from a troubled home life.

Educators do not wish to raise the ire of parents or to be accused of usurping parental authority. Many may fear that should they report to authorities about problems in a student's home, parents might instigate legal action against the school. Schools, like other organizations, are loath to become involved in litigation. Today, however, educators are protected from legal entanglements involving "good faith" reporting of health and safety problems among students. Nevertheless, past fears may still persist and act as a deterrent to educators who might otherwise want to intervene.

There are also many who believe that "risk diagnosis" is outside the realm of educators' professional duties and competencies. Ironically, many school staff feel it is quite appropriate to report a student's suspected medical or developmental difficulties which may contribute to learning problems, yet shy from involvement when it comes to personal crises which also affect learning. A truncated definition of school staff roles can hinder educators in taking appropriate action.

Some also fear that if educators talk about suicide, it will cause some students to attempt it. While there is much debate about such a possibility, our review of the research convinces us that this fear is unfounded. It is true that care must be taken in how educators approach the presentation to students of any materials related to suicide. There is no clear evidence, however, that a properly developed program or curriculum will cause an increase in suicidal thoughts or behaviors among students. To the contrary, most evidence suggests that a well-designed program presented by trained educators is likely to help identify students who may be prone to suicide. Nevertheless, as a consequence of assertions that suicide prevention programming in school will "give students bad ideas," some schools have been reluctant to do anything. We already know that inaction does not solve the problem.

Ironically, another reason for limited school involvement stems from the good intentions and helpful efforts of educators. School staff often refer potentially "at-risk" students to mental health or protective service agencies, but then become frustrated at what they perceive to be a lack of response. There are chronic complaints regarding poor communication between schools and agencies, lack of follow-up of reported cases, mismanagement of cases, and endless delays in providing assistance to troubled students and their families. The end result is a dangerous cynicism; school personnel simply give up on trying to make the system work.

From these observations, a simple conclusion can be drawn: schools have yet to realize their potential for lessening either the occurrence or the effects of youth suicide. That is not to say educators are uncaring. If anything, most are eager to help. But educators need resources and guidance in how to help. Educators are struggling to balance their academic responsibilities with the demand to solve serious social problems. Unless they are provided with the resources and guidance they need, they will be unable to effectively carry out their primary teaching mission.

Fortunately, there are hopeful signs. Many educators are taking the lead in community efforts to prevent youth suicide. Teachers, administrators, school nurses, school counselors and others are realizing a basic fact: in matters of health and safety, a student's family and peer affiliations are part of the educator's professional domain. This is especially true if a student is in physical danger or is suffering learning problems as a result of a family or personal crisis. Many educators correctly believe that as part of their role, they have both the right and the obligation to become involved.

The Educator's Role

We know that educators can play a critical role in addressing the problem of youth suicide. Coming to agreement as to the exact nature of that role, however, is not easy. The questions abound. Should teachers try to provide crisis intervention to high risk students? What role should educators allow students to play in implementing peer assistance programs? When do the responsibilities of community agencies and schools coincide and when do they clash? To what extent should parents be included in school programming? What kind of curriculum should schools introduce on suicide issues, and when should it be introduced? How can suicide prevention information be integrated into the curriculum? The list of questions goes on and on.

While the exact role of school personnel will vary from district to district, there are a number of areas which all schools should emphasize in marshaling efforts to address the problem. Schools should concentrate their attention on the following:

- establishing crisis response teams;

- developing policies and procedures to follow in the event of a suicide or attempted suicide;

- developing staff inservice training;

- identifying and referring high risk students;

- working with parents of high risk students;

- following up on cases referred to community agencies;

- fostering peer assistance programs;

- collaborating with mental health and other community agencies;

- incorporating primary prevention programming into the school curriculum which fosters in students the knowledge, values, and skills necessary for healthy lifestyles and good citizenship.

Because so many students need help, the potential contribution of schools in preventing suicide is enormous.

The student's right to protection should be a concern of every socially conscious educator. Concern alone, however, is not enough to solve the problem. Intelligent planning and action, based upon an understanding of the problem and training in how to deal with it, are required if educators and human service professionals are to achieve their potential in helping students in crisis.

2
UNDERSTANDING
STUDENTS IN CRISIS

What makes a young person want to take his or her life? The question becomes even more perplexing when we hear of bright, popular, and high achieving students who seemed to have everything going for them, yet they committed suicide. What happened? Why did they choose to die?

This question poses no easy answers. Some explanations place primary emphasis on personality factors, some emphasize predisposing environmental conditions, and still others stress the character of interaction between the person and the environment. But is there a common thread of understanding which explains what motivates a student to commit suicide?

Our review of the work of scholars, clinicians, and researchers on adolescent development, our review of the many theories of suicide, and our efforts to help students have caused us to believe that there is a common feature. Understanding adolescent suicide is not, as some have suggested, simply a matter of examining the character of depression, or stress, or family and peer relationships, or even personality deficits. True, these are important variables. But they are only important if understood in the context of one other critical variable — a pervasive sense of hopelessness.

THE IMPORTANCE OF HOPELESSNESS

The one common theme which ties together the vast majority of adolescent suicides is a pervasive sense of hopelessness in the face of seemingly overwhelming problems. Suicidal people have a compelling desire to escape from what they see as intolerable emotional pain. They are beset by what seems to them as intractable problems. They have no confidence that the future holds anything but more anger, stress, depression, or other forms of anguish. For them, the motive is not so much to die, but to escape from the condition of felt hopelessness.

A suicidal person's feelings of hopelessness usually arise when three conditions are present. First, the conditions of the person's life fall far short of what he or she believes to be necessary for happiness, and this is felt to be intolerable. Second, the person attributes some or all of the shortcomings or failures which are believed to be the source of unhappiness to personal inadequacies. Third, the person feels that nothing he or she does will make a difference — that the pain will continue and that he or she is powerless to make it abate.

Such conditions motivate a desire to escape, even if the method of escape is self-destruction. The person feels utterly hopeless. Coupled with this profound hopelessness among suicidal people is one or more of the following: severe depression, anger, guilt, or deep feelings of estrangement. The common theme is hopelessness, but the combination of conditions to which that hopelessness is attached will vary from person to person.

For example, a seriously depressed student who attempts suicide may not be angry; or an angry student may attempt suicide to "get even" with someone, yet not be clinically depressed. In either case, however, there is deep emotional turmoil which reflects a belief that the situation is absolutely intolerable. *Hopelessness in the face of a perceived intolerable situation usually is the catalyst for self-destruction — it is not depression, anger, guilt or estrangement per se that causes self-destruction.*

At one time or another most people experience painful events. Many people experience periods of depression, stress, loss, guilt or anger. Yet most are able to tolerate the pain without considering suicide. Why?

For most people, a willingness to tolerate pain, including intense physical or psychological pain, is predicated upon at least one of two conditions. First, tolerance for pain is possible if one believes that it is temporary. The thought that the pain will not endure makes it tolerable. But when people believe that there is no end to their suffering, and there is nothing else to compensate for their pain, then suicide may seem to be a viable solution. This is especially true for troubled young people who possess a truncated sense of what the future might be, and whose limited problem solving skills make it difficult for them to cope with immediate adversities.

The second condition which makes people willing to tolerate pain is often rooted in a core set of values concerned with the perceived needs of others who are important. Specifically, a set of values which gives one a mission to live because others would benefit, despite one's pain, is likely to deter suicide. An example would be a person with AIDS who refuses to give up because his or her efforts to bring health care to the terminally ill are an integral part of a cause greater than self. Another example is a teenager with a terminal disease who chooses not to commit suicide because such an act would bring hurt and shame on the family. Even though the pain is intense, with no hope of relief, the thought that others will benefit (or not be hurt) by one's struggle makes the pain tolerable. The bond to others, in spite of the pain, is a source of hope.

But when a young person feels hopeless in the face of what he or she believes is an intolerable problem, and this feeling of hopelessness is accompanied by severe depression, anger, guilt or estrangement, then the potential for self-destruction is high. Thus, in order to help potentially suicidal students, educators should understand something of the character of depression, anger, guilt, and estrangement in the context of feelings of hopelessness.

Depression

The basic emotional condition of severe depression is a prolonged and pervasive — almost obsessive — sadness. Depression can emerge for many reasons, some of which are not understood by either the individual or by professional observers. Regardless of the source, severe depression is one of the most dangerous conditions because of its impact on one's health, even if it does not cause suicide. If the person feels that even with the passage of time there is no hope of relief from this overwhelming sadness, then he or she may entertain suicidal thoughts.

The combination of hopelessness and severe depression in people can be deadly. The implication for those of us who work with students is clear. When we become aware of lethal circumstances (e.g., a seriously depressed student who feels hopeless, has a plan to commit suicide, and has the means to complete that plan), there should be no delay in our referral of the at-risk student to a trained specialist.

Anger

Coupled with hopelessness, an intense anger for felt wrongs done to self can contribute to a suicidal crisis when one believes that nothing one can do will make a difference to resolve the injustice. When people are angry at others for what has happened, and possibly angry at themselves for "allowing" themselves to be in such a situation, they often feel powerless. Yet their anger compels them to "do something." Tragically, the one way where intensely angry persons may find solace for their anger — where they see an end to the wrongs and a way to act which can punish someone — is through self-destruction. In this sense, an act of self-destruction is a way to end an injustice, a way to command power, or a way to gain revenge.

Guilt

There are parallels between anger and guilt. In the context of suicide, both are associated with hopelessness and with feelings that a wrong was committed, and both can drive one to take extreme actions. A key difference, however, is that anger is associated with an imputed wrong by others, while guilt involves self-blame. For example, if a student is upset over receiving a failing grade, an angry response is to blame the teacher for being unfair. In contrast, a guilty response is to blame one's self for the poor grade.

Some have argued that guilt is anger directed inward, and suicide that is the result of overwhelming guilt is really an act of murder . . . the victim is murdering the one who is to blame for the wrong. In such a case, it is argued that suicide is an act of self-punishment rather than revenge.

From our vantage point, there is no way to test the accuracy of such conjecture. Yet a consideration of guilt as an element in adolescent suicide suggests to us two arguments which are supported by research.

Many therapists whose clients are child and adolescent survivors of physical or sexual abuse find that these clients experience deep feelings of guilt and shame. We believe that this is an outcome of two interrelated conditions: these victims have learned to feel responsible for what has happened, and their relatively powerless position means that they are not allowed to feel or to express anger toward those who are the source of the wrong. They are also in a position where they cannot prevent being continually abused, and they blame themselves for this presumed failure. This is illustrated by the example of an incest victim who still loves her offending father. The child says to herself: "I love my dad and I don't have the right to be angry with him. I must be to blame for what has happened." Such attribution of guilt to self, when viewed in the face of an intolerable and hopeless situation, can drive one to attempt suicide.

Another way in which guilt is important to our understanding of suicide centers on a troubled person's definitions of self. A common manifestation of both guilt and shame is very low self-esteem. The person feels utterly worthless, in large part because the undesirable conditions of life are seen as due to some personal inadequacy or failure. These feelings of worthlessness are made even worse if the person is also being stigmatized by others. The person's self-definitions are expressed by adjectives such as "bad," "incompetent," "inadequate," "defective," "inept," "unlikable," and "unlovable."

Furthermore, these negative self-definitions among suicidal persons take on a "global" character. They learn to perceive themselves as worthless in nearly all of their roles and relationships, and not merely in a single arena. When coupled with feelings of hopelessness, these attributions of self as worthless, incompetent, and unlovable — as guilty of being a hopeless failure with no future — can motivate suicidal behavior.

Estrangement

Estrangement is the feeling of being isolated from others. There are at least four distinct types of estrangement which are relevant to our understanding of adolescent suicide. The first type is characterized as a disaffection or indifference toward one's social environment and is accompanied by self withdrawal. In such cases, one's most salient values, beliefs, interests and concerns seem to be at odds with those of nearly all others with whom one is in contact. Reasons for such disaffection are wide-ranging and may be exacerbated by class, religious, racial, or other distinctions. Whatever the source of this estrangement, the result is that the person *voluntarily* withdraws from social contacts. This self-induced isolation in turn means that there is no one to turn to in times of personal crisis when one experiences profound feelings of hopelessness.

The second type of estrangement is imposed by others. Terms such as "ostracize" and "outcast" capture the essence of this isolation from others. It is not so much that the person wants to be excluded. Rather, he or she has no choice — others simply avoid the person, or worse, actively seek to humiliate him or her. These persons bear the stigma and humiliation of public rejection. Examples include students who are bullied or who are openly identified by their peers as "nerds." To further compound the problem, when people are stigmatized in the eyes of others, it fundamentally affects their views of self. The net effect of being shunned is that the person is physically and psychologically isolated from others, while at the same time holding a very low sense of self-esteem.

A third form of estrangement is based upon distorted perceptions of self-worth. This might best be called estrangement from self. Some students learn to define their value — both in their own eyes and in the eyes of others — strictly in terms of what they *do* and not who they *are*. In other words, they see themselves, or believe they are seen by significant others, as valued only for their extrinsic rather than their intrinsic worth.

For these students, self-worth is directly linked to their achievements. They are often perfectionistic, high-achieving and driven students who possess a deep fear of failure. Failure for them — even if it is only what others might see as minor transgressions — is translated into an intolerable loss of love, approval, and validation. These students are isolated not in the objective sense of either voluntary withdrawal or ostracism, but in the subjective sense of feeling fear in the face of possible failure. In fact, many are often popular "stars" in their schools, which in turn may add to their felt pressure to perform. Yet regardless of whether these excessively high performance expectations come from significant others or are self-imposed, such students are in a constant state of performance anxiety. The pressure to maintain "perfection" in order to feel worthy can precipitate in them profound feelings of isolation and hopelessness; they become suicidal either in anticipation of some failure, or in the face of an actual setback.

The fourth type of estrangement associated with suicide is implied in the term "anomie." Here the person has no predictable or consistent sense of belonging to a community of others. The person feels profoundly alone in an alien environment. Such feelings of isolation or estrangement often are an outcome of being uprooted from one social system and placed in another where none of the former rules of life seem to apply. This state of disaffection is made worse by what is a seeming breakdown of clear social norms, or by the young person's limited means of coping with (or even anticipating) the complex demands of a new system. Simply stated, the person has no sense of community from which to derive guidance or support.

One example is a juvenile being removed from family and school, and then being placed in jail for the first time. Another common example is a student whose family moves frequently; he or she is constantly uprooted and placed in new schools with little time or support for adjustment. Under such circumstances, feelings of uncertainty and insecurity can pervade virtually all aspects of one's life. In this new environment, the former rules of life are abandoned, yet it is uncertain how one can meet the new demands which one confronts. For seriously troubled young people with marginal coping skills, the result is feeling hopelessly isolated from lines of support at a time of great unpredictability.

Some scholars believe that dramatic social changes, especially those that are sweeping families and communities, are a major source of anomie among our young. They believe that many of our youth are growing up in families and communities that fail to offer even the most rudimentary guidance and support. Where neglect, violence, and lawlessness prevail, so too does estrangement from others. This in turn sets the stage for suicide when one's situation is felt to be hopeless and unbearable.

In each of these cases — depression, anger, guilt and estrangement — the common theme is a sense of hopelessness in the face of intolerable circumstances. Because these conditions are not mutually exclusive, the more that each is present, the greater the sense of hopelessness. It is hopelessness and the unbearableness of pain that are the basis of suicide risk among our young.

To reduce suicide risk among students, the goal is obvious: instill in them feelings of hope and the skills to cope with problems. Although more will be said about this in a later chapter, in practical terms this means teaching students the knowledge and skills to build a community of support, to avoid social isolation, to develop healthy self-images, and to resolve personal crises.

For most students who experience difficulties, their families, friends, schools and churches help them in ways which reduce the risk of suicide. But many still fall through the cracks. Some high risk students give off few (if any) clear indications that they are suicide prone. To others, they look like "winners." Nevertheless, the majority of students who attempt suicide usually provide some clues as to their intentions. As educators, therefore, our task is to learn to recognize and attend to such urgent clues.

3
RECOGNIZING
PREDISPOSING CONDITIONS

A profound state of hopelessness in a suicidal student seldom emerges spontaneously. Most often it develops over a period of weeks, months or years, gradually emerging out of chronically troublesome conditions in the young person's life. Early identification of these conditions is central to the mission of reducing the potential for suicide. Preventing suicidal behavior in students is much easier if educators learn to recognize problematic conditions which may ultimately manifest themselves in acts of self-destruction.

Early identification of problems which may or may not eventually produce suicidal behavior, however, is not the same task as that of screening students who already are at high risk of suicide. *Early identification means the recognition of any potentially debilitating condition which could seriously impair the health or competencies of a student.* Screening for suicidal behavior, on the other hand, is much more specific in focus. Yet the task of identifying students who experience those conditions which may provoke suicidal behavior is easier said than done. The difficulty of early identification in schools is threefold.

- Educators seldom know much about the important relationships their students have with their families, friends, or others.

- Troubled youth rarely intentionally identify themselves; they usually live with their pain rather than seek the help of adults at school.

- Finally, few educators have had sufficient training to recognize the background conditions and the early stages of emotional and behavioral patterns characteristic of students who are likely to eventually experience a suicidal crisis.

To compound the problem, the professional literature suggests seemingly contradictory characteristics for those who may become at risk of suicide. Some are said to "act out" while others are "withdrawn;" some are said to be "compulsive achievers" while others are "underachievers;" some are said to exhibit "flattened emotions" while others display inappropriately "exaggerated emotions;" and on and on. Anyone can be confused when presented with such profiles.

What these profiles do make clear, however, is that people who are at risk of intentionally harming themselves are not all alike. A particular symptom will appear in some but not in others. In addition, an emotional or behavioral pattern may occur at one point in time but not at another. Finally, the same signs may arise from a variety of situations. For example, child abuse, sexual assault, and substance abuse each can generate similar symptoms, even though the character of the interventions appropriate for each problem will vary.

To additionally compound the problem of recognizing predisposing conditions, it is common to attribute many of the early warning signs exhibited by young people to their youthful status, rather than to their experiencing a suicidal or other serious crisis. Because many adults expect young people to behave in ways which do not conform to adult norms, genuine signs of trouble can be mistaken for being an "adolescent phase."

Given the difficulties of early problem identification, what can we reasonably expect to do? Educators cannot be expected to accurately test each student for every possible malady, including suicide potential. It is likewise unreasonable to require teachers and other school staff to have expertise in clinical symptomatology. However, educators can and should be able to assess for problems which increase the *possibility* of certain students being at high risk, and then make referrals accordingly. With respect to suicide, for example, educators need to be able to identify and refer students who *might* be suicidal. Might is the key word; it is not the task of educators to say which students *are* suicidal. Rather, educators only need to be reasonably suspicious to make referrals to professionals trained in clinical assessment and suicide intervention.

In order to make reasonably based referrals, however, educators need proper training in early identification of student problems. They need to be able to recognize the initial stages of both situational and personal attributes which eventually may undermine the health or competencies of their students. The presence of these attributes can set the stage for gradual deterioration; thus, early identification is critical in order to prevent decline into suicidal hopelessness. Teachers and other school staff should report their observations when they note in their students severely limited coping skills, unrealistic perceptions, extreme behavioral problems, or serious developmental delay.

Developmental Delay

Significant developmental delays in students often suggest a raft of serious problems. Such delays are especially relevant when observing younger students who seem to lag far behind their peers academically or socially. Developmental delay in cognitive or in social skills can result from genetics, birth trauma, or accidents. It can also stem from child maltreatment. Unfortunately, a seriously dysfunctional home can affect the acquisition of academic and social skills, and is often associated with students who later attempt self-destruction.

Emotional and Behavioral Maladjustment

An emotional maladjustment is when one's feelings consistently impair one's ability to function. An array of emotional problems, from being extremely sullen and withdrawn to a constant state of being "up," can impair student abilities to behave in acceptable ways. This is particularly true in cases where students cannot appropriately adjust to novel shifts in their situations. Their maladjustments may include extreme and irrational fear of people, dramatic emotional outbursts and mood swings, being affectively "stuck" or displaying inappropriate affect, and exhibiting an inability to trust those deserving of trust.

Because emotional maladjustments often lead to problem behaviors, most educators are alert to indications that a student is acting inappropriately toward classmates or others. Educators also should note other signs in their students such as poor attention span, lack of cooperativeness, substance abuse, violence, serious displays of disrespect for legitimate authority, and so forth. Although these signs often indicate emotional distress, caution is necessary. We should not depend only on problem behavior to identify students with severe emotional problems. Many students in emotional turmoil do not openly manifest behavioral problems. Some even appear to be model students.

One typical behavioral problem which often escapes the attention of educators from preschool through higher education, is compulsive overconformity. For example, a compulsive achiever may forgo sleep to the point of complete exhaustion in order to accomplish some end which he or she sees as critical, though others do not. On the surface, such a student seemingly poses less difficulties than one who constantly exhibits negative behaviors. Yet overconformity can be an indication of serious dysfunction, especially when there is panic and extreme self-criticism at even minor failures.

Compulsiveness in high achievement may be a way of gaining a measure of control over uncertainty in one's life, and it can be a way of pleasing others. Some suicidal students are very popular with their peers — some are "stars." Such students may feel compelled as a result of their being popular to do even more to please or to help their many friends, even if this leads to self-harm.

On the surface, these students seem incredibly mature because they willingly assume responsibilities, often to the point of excess. This may make them feel resentful. However, they may not express their resentment because they feel compelled to hold everything together for their families or others, but not for themselves.

There is a real danger for educators who encounter compulsively overconforming students. The danger is that because these students seem so mature and responsible, there will be a tendency to give them even more responsibilities. And these pupils inevitably will accept new responsibilities, even if they are driven to the brink.

On the other end of the continuum from compulsiveness to achieve is a compulsiveness to fail. Students driven to failure are unable to assume any appropriate responsibility. These students seemingly reject or ignore almost all demands placed on them, including the most reasonable requests. They seemingly care little for the quality of their school work. They usually have very poor self-images, in part because they can claim few worthy accomplishments. This in turn makes it even more difficult for them to accept responsibility or to care.

One result is that these students are seldom popular with either their peers or with their teachers. They retreat from nearly all demands, and in turn, little comes to be expected of them. They "foul up," which causes them to be treated with indifference or disdain, which causes them to "foul up" even more.

Unrealistic Perceptions

Some students seem unable to change their behaviors, even when it is clear that their actions are harmful to themselves. They seem to lack the ability to assess what is happening to them. When told by others what is wrong, such well-intentioned advice often is ignored or misinterpreted. Even in the face of unequivocal evidence that they are overextended, in poor health, or alienating everyone around them, these students do not stop what they are doing. Many students who become suicidal suffer from the inability to be realistic in regard to the obvious. They fail to recognize and to change the very behaviors which eventually create in them the intent to end their lives.

A Felt Lack of Coping Skills

Often linked to unrealistic perceptions is a lack of reasonable judgment and a lack of effective communication skills. These students experience great frustration because their attempts to manage problems fail. In a sense, the source of their felt frustration is not necessarily the problem *per se,* but rather their belief that they lack the ability to resolve their problems. This further reinforces in them feelings of hopelessness.

For those students with a felt lack of coping abilities, there is usually a common denominator: they have not had access to others who would teach them how to solve problems. They usually lack good role models. Many of these students have only negative peer or adult role models who reinforce poor coping skills. As a result, when confronted with difficulties, these students make poor choices, and then fail to communicate to those who could help.

Harmful Relationships

Being sensitive to a lack of coping skills, unrealistic perceptions about things that matter, emotional maladjustments or delays in development lead us to look at the character of the interactions students have with others. One of the most significant categories of interaction in the lives of students can be seen in the way they relate to their parents. There is ample evidence that maltreatment of children is closely linked to both childhood and adulthood problems, including suicide.

There are types of dysfunctional parent-child interaction patterns that place children at very high risk throughout their lives. A family history of child physical or sexual abuse, or a history of parental alcoholism with all the attendant family dysfunctions, are potent predisposing conditions for self-destruction. In such families, the development in children of feelings of powerlessness and shame can lead to suicidal hopelessness.

What does this imply? For educators, training in identification of child abuse and neglect is critical if subsequent problems are to be avoided. Educators also should be alert to clues such as young students who appear to be taking care of their parents or younger siblings, and who assume parent-like functions in the family which are well beyond their capacity to handle. This often occurs not only in cases of neglect and parental alcoholism, but also in the wake of a divorce.

Educators should likewise take note of those parents and students who only communicate in the most constricted and functional manner. They literally never have a meaningful conversation. Their communication is limited to simple declaratives such as "Turn off the TV" or "Clean up your room." Such communication, which is almost totally devoid of positive affect, usually signals problems.

Any clue of serious parent-child problems should sensitize educators to the possibility that a student may need to be seen by an expert in assessing high-risk individuals. However, educators should look for *repeated patterns,* not isolated behaviors, in making judgments about referral and other interventions.

Dysfunctional relationships and related maladaptive behaviors often have the effect of isolating students from caring adults. In the worst cases, the result is estrangement, guilt, intense anger, or severe depression which could lead to suicidal hopelessness. When educators encounter such students, it is essential to bring them to the attention of those who can help. Recognizing signs of acute distress which impair the competencies of students, followed by the provision of timely interventions, should be the concern of every educator.

RECOGNIZING ACUTE STRESS

Broadly speaking, the emergence of a suicidal crisis implies a progressive deterioration which includes intense thoughts and fantasies about suicide, and suicide plans. This is most clearly manifest when we observe suicide attempts of various degrees of lethality. Whenever there is knowledge or suspicion about a student having thoughts and plans for suicide, school personnel must immediately refer that person to a professional who is trained to conduct a thorough assessment.

For some, the sense of hopelessness emerges gradually with the progression of a mental or physical disorder (e.g., schizophrenia). For others, the onset of hopelessness is rapid. In either case, the coping strategies of the student become so eroded by feelings of hopelessness that suicide is seen as perhaps the only way

out. The task for persons in contact with students is to be
alert to those conditions likely to produce the acute stress
which can lead to feelings of suicidal hopelessness. The
following box lists situational events which can foster in
students acute stress, and subsequently a sense of
hopelessness associated with self-destructive thoughts and
behaviors.

Situational Conditions

★ The death of a family member or close friend.

★ Anniversary dates of painful life events such as the death of a parent or other loved one.

★ Tough transition times (e.g., parents' divorce, breakup with dating partner, severe dread of "real world" following graduation, loss of valued peer relationship, transferring to a new school).

★ Being socially isolated (i.e., the lack of close personal relationships).

★ Involvement in blended family relationships where there is frequent and serious conflict with stepparent or siblings.

★ Chronic and intensifying conflicts with parents, employers, teachers or peers.

★ Prolonged presence in a pathological family (e.g., parental substance abuse, incest, family violence).

★ The onset of severe illness or disability in self or a family member, with little hope of improvement.

★ For the disabled or seriously ill, the worsening of the disability or pain (or fear of progressive deterioration), especially when coupled with the discouragement of the medical personnel or the withdrawal of treatment or support services.

★ The experience (or anticipated experience) of significant failure or embarrassment (e.g., flunking; being bullied in front of others).

★ The loss of a job or other valued role.

★ Incarceration or other significant trouble with the law.

★ Serious alcohol or other drug abuse (this may be a symptom of depression as well as a condition producing depression).

★ Confirmation of an unwanted pregnancy, especially before parents or peers find out.

★ When one is forced to assume significant responsibilities but lacks the emotional resources and skills to do so.

★ Intense and relentless emphasis by others (e.g., parents) on one's achievement, coupled with the fear of disapproval for failure to achieve.

★ Conflicts over one's emerging sexual identity or preference.

Students vary considerably in their coping skills when confronting the conditions listed. For some, these events can produce such acute emotional distress that profound feelings of hopelessness emerge. In addition, the negative or rejecting responses of others to one's attempts to cope often exacerbate feelings of hopelessness.

In the face of precipitating stressful conditions, most people never reach the stage where they commit suicide. Unfortunately, others act to self-destruct. As we have noted, some who are intent upon suicide do not always act in ways which alert even trained therapists. For most young people at risk, however, there are verbal and behavioral clues for recognizing personal crises.

Many experts believe that the majority — perhaps as many as nine-out-of-ten young people who commit suicide — give prior clues as to their intentions. Such clues usually are exhibited in *patterns* rather than as isolated symptoms. Our knowledge of these patterned verbal and behavioral indicators, especially those associated with acute depression, guilt, anger or estrangement, will help to identify students who should be referred for more careful assessment. These indicators among students are listed in the following box.

Personal Conditions

★ There are marked changes in behavior. These may include changes in sleeping habits, the onset of eating disorders (including dramatic weight gain or loss), extreme promiscuity, dramatic emotional outbursts, uncharacteristic acts of rebellion, or dramatic decline in school performance.

★ There is voluntary isolation from friends and withdrawal from normally sociable activities.

★ There is a significant increase in use of alcohol or other drugs.

★ There is neglect of personal appearance.

★ There is sometimes senseless risk-taking or clear lack of concern for personal welfare.

★ There is an exaggeration of health complaints or the emergence of psychosomatic illnesses.

★ There is a pronounced difficulty in being able to concentrate on tasks (often coupled with dramatic mood changes).

★ There is a preoccupation with death, with morbid thoughts or with themes of destruction.

★ There are expressions of pervasive and enduring sadness, or there are expressions of inappropriate affect (bursts of laughter or crying which do not fit with the social context).

★ There are serious distortions in perceptions of reality.

★ There is an inability to make even the most minor decisions.

★ There is very low self-esteem.

★ There is preoccupation with escape fantasies.

★ There is intense anger or desire for revenge against real or imagined enemies.

★ There is behavior that is characterized by trying to put one's life in order (e.g., giving away possessions and settling accounts).

★ There is constant seeking of attention through inappropriate behaviors.

★ There are suicide threats or attempts to commit suicide.

When a pattern of clues emerges, and it is linked to feelings of hopelessness coupled with depression, guilt, anger, or estrangement, suicide is a clear possibility. For the suicidal student, hopelessness is a motivating force behind these thoughts, feelings, and behaviors. However, it is important for educators to understand that most students who are having difficulties do not seek to resolve them via suicide. In fact, most young people are reasonably well-adjusted and able to cope, even when they confront potentially devastating problems. They may not have mastered all of the problem solving skills for coping with the myriad challenges presented to them, but most do manage.

On the other hand, some come to feel that their lives are hopeless and that a better future is unattainable. It is they who most need help. With appropriate assessment and referral, suicide can be prevented. Sadly, so often in the case of adolescent suicide, people recognize in retrospect the pattern of problems and the resultant state of hopelessness that had previously escaped their attention. For those students who are at highest risk, therefore, educators need to accomplish two basic objectives: develop crisis response teams, and adopt a systematic means of screening students for suicide potential.

4
DEVELOPING CRISIS
RESPONSE TEAMS

Educators helping troubled students — especially when working in isolation from other professionals — often feel overwhelmed. Many simply "burn out," including those with a talent for helping. Clearly, no single professional can serve all students in need.

One way to increase the capacity of educators to help is to share responsibilities via a school-based crisis response team. The operation of these teams should be a key element in the district's crisis response plans used by schools in the aftermath of a tragedy (e.g., accidental death, suicide, murder) affecting students or staff. Our experience with crisis teams, as well as the observations of many other experts (Barrett, 1987; Ruof and Harris, 1988a; Ruof, Harris, and Robbie, 1987; Steele, 1992), suggest that the team concept has the following advantages:

- provides each team member with a support system;

- gives students access to multiple helpers;

- allows for shared responsibilities;

- increases the likelihood that vulnerable students will not have to wait to receive help;

- enhances the power of decisions made since recommendations come from a group of professionals;

- encourages swift resolution of the crisis;

- improves the school's ability to monitor student behavior;

- ensures an organized response to a traumatic event;

- reduces the likelihood of liability;

- enhances opportunities to train students and staff.

We believe that these benefits outweigh the modest financial costs of staff training for good reason: a team increases the probability of help being available, while reducing the potential of a mishandled crisis. In our litigious society, schools cannot afford to NOT have a crisis team. Thus, the first step in creating a crisis response team is to gain administrative support.

Gaining Administrative Support

Despite the advantages of having a crisis response team, it is sometimes difficult to convince school boards and administrators to allocate scarce monetary and staff resources for team development. Ruof and her colleagues (1987, 1988a) and Poland (1989) make a number of helpful suggestions to elicit support from the school administration.

First, provide administrators and others with information about the rate of teenage suicide at the national, state, and local levels. Gathering data on the number of local threats, attempts, and completions can be compelling evidence to counter the claims of those who deny that a problem exists in their district. It is also important to dispel common myths about teenage suicide such as: "Talking about it makes it happen," "You can't change a person's mind once they've decided to commit suicide," and "Adolescents threatening suicide are manipulative; ignoring them is the best thing to do."

Second, emphasize the legal responsibility to intervene with high-risk students. Administrators need to know that they may be liable for *failure* to take appropriate action in the event of a crisis. In Kelson *vs.* The City of Springfield (1985), the court held that parents of a deceased child can bring action against the school if the death was the result of inadequate staff training in suicide prevention. Reluctant administrators should be urged to consult the school district's attorney if there is no program or plan.

Third, discuss the advantages of a team approach, including the ability of team members to fashion crisis intervention policies, and to train staff and students in identification and referral skills. Explain the concept of suicide contagion, and how a trained team can reduce the possibility of contagion in the aftermath of a traumatic event. Emphasize that doing nothing for students in crisis will produce resentment from the community and adverse media coverage. Conversely, having a trained team suggests that both the school administration and staff are proactive, competent, and compassionate.

Finally, provide examples of how schools with crisis teams have helped to save lives and reduce the risk of contagion after a student's death. If possible, select examples from schools which are geographically close.

If administrators or school boards still remain resistant to having a team, Ruof and Harris (1988a) suggest calling these individuals whenever a staff member is dealing with a suicidal student. They found that keeping key decision makers apprised of the demand for crisis services, particularly when the crisis occurs on the weekend or at 2:00 A.M., can be a significant motivator for action.

Team Structure

Once committed to developing a crisis team, school personnel must then decide upon a team model which can receive wide endorsement. Ruof and Harris (1988b) consider three different crisis team models currently being used. The *Building Level Team* is comprised of staff who work daily in a particular building; it includes regular and special education teachers, administrators, coaches, and counselors. The advantages of this model include the following: (1) members know the staff and students more intimately than would professionals from outside the school, and may be able to develop better rapport with high risk students; (2) the team is readily available when a crisis occurs; (3) referrals are made more easily and earlier because members work in the building; (4) team members can provide ongoing support to at-risk students; and (5) members are available to observe changes in student behavior over time.

The *District Level Team* is comprised of professionals from local helping agencies, as well as district school psychologists, social workers, instructional consultants, or nurses who are employed by schools within the district.

The advantages are that these professionals usually have: (1) appropriate clinical skills; (2) experience handling students in crisis; (3) can influence decision-makers in the school system; and (4) are linked to helping resources in the community.

The third model is the *Combined Team* which has both building level representatives, district representatives, and community representatives as needed. Ruof and Harris favor the Combined Team for a number of reasons. This arrangement offers the advantage of having building level members who are immediately available to initiate appropriate interventions for at-risk students, to evaluate the effect of these interventions, and to provide on-going support and follow-up to students needing help. District staff and community representatives, because of their training with crisis assessment and intervention, also can provide support and supervision for building team members, as well as consultation on cases. Finally, having a Combined Team increases the probability that enough trained people will be available in the event of a tragedy.

Having worked with all three kinds of teams, we also strongly endorse the Combined Team model. Our experience is that in the case of a strictly Building Level Team, the team agenda often becomes subsumed under the daily demands of staff as they carry out their roles. So too have we found that a strictly District Level Team is often removed from the intimate details of students' lives — useful knowledge during a crisis that building staff possess. The Combined Team Model avoids these disadvantages through the sharing of resources and expertise. It also works well in small or rural districts where, in a crisis, schools must rely on staff from community agencies for additional help.

Team Composition

Once school personnel decide upon a team structure, they must decide how many team members to train. Ruof and Harris (1988b) recommend one team member for every 100 children, with each building having a minimum of two members. Poland and Pitcher (1990) recommend 4-8 team members per school district. Steele (1992) states that 7 or 8 members for the district will maximize the benefits of the team process.

If resources permit, our recommendation is to have 3-5 trained team members in *each building within the district*. The principal of each building would preferably be on the team, or would at least be giving it full backing. If principals are uninterested or uninvolved, faculty may not be supportive. Team members from each building would then be part of a larger team for the whole district comprised of building, district, and community professionals. All or part of the team could be used, depending on the nature of the problem and the number of students affected. For instance, a fatal bus accident involving students from several schools within the district would require using the entire team. On the other hand, the suicide of a well-known and popular parent of an elementary child might use only the team members in that elementary school to handle the crisis.

Recruitment of Team Members

In recruiting for team membership, only school professionals with the characteristics of warmth, sensitivity, and strong interpersonal skills should be considered. These are the staff most likely to be approached by students. Other characteristics to look for include stability, maturity, good judgment, ability to handle stress and confrontation, and having a solid support system (Ruof & Harris, 1988b). It may also be important to select members with flexibility in their daily schedules in order to accommodate crisis work with students and parents. However, simply assigning team members based upon the sole criterion of availability (rather than interest and ability) is an ineffective approach.

Before joining a team, school personnel should be informed of the training requirements and of their duties. They should also be informed of the voluntary nature of team membership, any compensation or incentives members might receive, and the limits of team responsibility. Ruof and Harris (1988b) add that potential members have the right to know how much support and supervision they can expect from more experienced team members and from the district's administrators. They also state that team members always should have the right to decline involvement if they so choose. Having fearful or unwilling members can sabotage the team process.

Training Members

All team members should receive training at the same time. This allows the team to develop a common frame of reference and builds cohesion. Obviously, the length of training will vary depending on the previous training and experience of team members. Ruof and Harris (1988b) recommend as much as 30 hours of training with recertification credit for participation. Steele (1992) suggests that members receive two full days of training, and an additional 12 hours (3 half-day sessions) during the first three months of operation. Barrett (1987) recommends a minimum of 8 hours of training. Whatever the duration of training, the important thing is for team members to feel prepared to address the problems they may encounter.

Our recommendation is to conduct an initial two day training (16 hours) with yearly half-day or full-day booster sessions. In addition, for the first three months following the initial training, we recommend that the team should meet twice per month for at least one hour, and monthly thereafter. These meetings should focus on: (1) practicing new skills through role play; (2) clarifying responsibilities of team members; (3) reviewing crisis response policies and procedures; (4) coordinating services among buildings; (5) reviewing cases, particularly those that went smoothly or were especially problematic; (6) developing a plan to train new members; (7) evaluating services already provided; (8) identifying problem areas and resolving these; and (9) strengthening group cohesiveness (Ruof & Harris, 1988b; Steele, 1992).

Training should be conducted by experienced professionals, particularly those from the local community who have expertise in crisis assessment and intervention with adolescents (Steele, 1992). It is also important to contract with persons who have conducted training sessions in the past, and who can effectively teach the requisite material. If expense is a concern, one option is to send selected school personnel for extensive training, and then ask these professionals to provide training to district staff (Poland, 1989). Effective training sessions are usually both didactic and experiential, including the use of lectures, audio-visual materials, self-evaluation exercises, small group discussions and exercises, case histories, and guided role play (Ryerson, 1987a). The training information we recommend for crisis team members is indicated in the following box. Once members are trained, they should carry out prevention, intervention, and postvention responsibilities.

Content of Training

Comprehensive training for crisis response team members should include the following:

★ national, state, and local statistics on adolescent suicide;

★ exploration of trainees' feelings and attitudes regarding suicide and the school's role in suicide prevention;

★ team structure, roles, and responsibilities;

★ team-building exercises;

★ societal, community, family, peer, and other factors contributing to youth suicide;

★ myths and facts about those at risk;

★ dynamics of the suicidal crisis, especially the conditions associated with hopelessness;

★ warning signs and identifying students at-risk;

★ crisis communication with high-risk youth;

★ active listening skills;

★ risk assessment skills;

★ crisis intervention skills following assessment;

★ crisis interview techniques with resistant or angry parents;

★ referral resources and procedures;

★ appropriate documentation of assessment and intervention procedures;

★ legal and ethical issues, including guidelines for confidentiality;

★ follow-up procedures with high-risk students;

★ postvention planning in the aftermath of a tragedy;

★ grief resolution following a death, with attention to developmental differences in expressions of grief among students of various ages;

★ debriefing strategies which facilitate recovery for students and staff following a death;

★ prevention of suicide contagion;

★ media guidelines for postvention;

★ teaching identification and referral skills to school staff, students, and parents.

Prevention Responsibilities

The crisis response team is in an ideal position to help administrators develop district-wide policies and procedures for suicide prevention and intervention. They also have an important role in shaping a postvention plan to be used in the aftermath of a tragedy. Following policy development, the team can train staff, students, and parents in identification and referral skills. The team also can help to identify conditions which place certain students at risk, and develop programming to help these students.

Intervention Responsibilities

Team members would be responsible for conducting preliminary screening of those students who appear to be at high risk of suicide or who are otherwise exhibiting seriously dysfunctional behaviors, and then would develop intervention plans for those students. Because team members often act as the liaison to community agencies which provide services to high-risk students, it is important for team members to secure detailed information about these resources, and to cultivate a working relationship with agency personnel. Team members are also in the best position to provide follow-up at school for those students referred to community agencies.

Postvention Responsibilities

In the event of a tragedy, the team would be responsible for coordinating and implementing the postvention plan. As part of this plan, team members would provide debriefing and support services to students and to staff. They would also provide information to parents about helping their children through the grieving process. Team members would make contact with the parents of students who most need help in the aftermath of a tragedy. Their role is to provide parents with information about available school and community resources, answer questions, and be available to help if needed.

Coordinator Responsibilities

Each crisis response team should have a district level and a building level coordinator. The district team coordinator would trouble-shoot regarding district suicide prevention policies and procedures. She or he would arrange for the training of staff, students, and parents in suicide prevention. In addition, the district coordinator would schedule and run team meetings, organize periodic booster skills training for team members, and recruit new members as needed. In the event of a crisis, she or he would call the team together, assign tasks, and monitor the effectiveness of the team in carrying out its responsibilities. The district coordinator would also oversee debriefing sessions for the team in the days and weeks following a tragedy.

The responsibility of the building level coordinator is to link high-risk students to crisis response team members for assessment and intervention. The building coordinator is also responsible for monitoring referral, parent notification, and follow-up procedures following the assessment of students. In the event of a tragedy, she or he would act as spokesperson for the team while directing the activities of team members at the building site.

Ongoing Team Training

Regularly scheduled training and supervision of team members is essential for maintaining a viable team. As discussed previously, we recommend yearly half-day or full-day booster sessions for team members. In addition, we recommend holding team meetings once a month for at least the first year following team training, and a minimum of four team meetings each year in subsequent years. Without these meetings, members can lose their team identity and be unprepared to work together in the event of a crisis. Attendance at these meetings should be a priority. Although occasional absences can be expected, repeated absences of one member will make it difficult for other members to trust and support that person (Steele, 1992).

Regular meetings are particularly helpful for evaluating the impact of intervention efforts conducted by the team. Steele (1992) likens the sharing of assessment, intervention, and follow-up after a crisis to "on the job" training for members. Learning from an actual intervention is far more powerful than reviewing training materials or even role playing simulated crises.

Steele also emphasizes the importance of debriefing team members following a crisis. Debriefing provides team members with the opportunity to talk about their reactions following the crisis, and to receive support and validation from others. It also provides an opportunity to process what worked and what did not, and to develop a plan for revising unsuccessful approaches. The longer the team members have unresolved doubts about the intervention, the less effective they will be in subsequent interventions and the faster they will burn out.

It is important that team members respect confidentiality concerning issues discussed in team meetings. If members think their behavior, ideas, or feelings will be talked about outside the team, they will be reluctant to attend or to honestly review what took place, especially after less than favorable interventions.

STAFF TRAINING

The effectiveness of a crisis response team depends upon support from others in school — especially the teachers — who are in direct contact with students and their parents. After a crisis response team is formed, it is therefore critical that teachers and other staff receive training in identifying and referring students to the team.

Teachers usually appreciate training which will allow them to be more effective in working with students, including those at risk of suicide. For example, Boggs (1987) found that 92% of elementary and 100% of secondary teachers trained in suicide prevention recommended that all teachers receive this information. Teachers reported increased knowledge of warning signs, as well as how to get help for youth in crisis.

Ryerson and King (1986) emphasize three reasons for training school staff in suicide prevention. First, teachers and other school personnel are less resistant to recognizing warning signs than parents who may deny the intensity and seriousness of their child's crisis. Second, unlike students, school staff are less constrained by peer loyalty or confidentiality conflicts in making referrals to helping professionals. Third, teachers have had extensive experience working with "average" students, so they often can sense when one is in trouble.

Our own observations point to additional advantages in training school staff. Because teachers spend so much time with their students, they are in an excellent position to recognize dysfunctional changes in behavior and other signs indicative of a crisis. In addition, without educating school personnel in identification skills, the crisis response team may get few referrals of high-risk youth. In such cases, they may end up spending little time preventing student problems, and much more time responding after a tragedy has occurred. Finally, given a litigious climate, schools without trained school staff run a significant risk of being sued by parents should a suicide occur.

Staff Training Logistics

Several decisions should be made before providing suicide prevention training to school staff. The first decision is whether staff training will be voluntary or involuntary. Our recommendation is to require all staff to attend in-service training on this topic. During training, however, it is important to be sensitive to the stress the subject might generate in some (e.g., survivors, previous attempters), and make preparations to help such persons after the presentation if necessary. It is also important to acknowledge at the beginning of the training that some staff might feel anxious discussing the topic. It should be stressed that given the dramatic increase in adolescent suicide, it is essential for all school staff to know how to identify and refer high-risk youth. Emphasizing the role of school personnel in preventing student suicide, and empowering them with the belief that they can make a difference, will help reduce potential staff resistance to the training.

Another concern is who shall receive training. We strongly recommend that all school personnel receive at least some training, including administrators, teachers, coaches, bus drivers, secretaries, food service workers, custodians, and auxiliary personnel. The roles school staff play are diverse, and the opportunity to observe potentially at-risk students in a variety of settings increases when everyone is trained. For example, a bus driver or a coach may be able to observe student behaviors which are quite different from those observed by teachers.

If possible, we suggest limiting group size to no more than 25-30 school professionals during the training. Having a group of this size or smaller allows for more discussion than will occur in larger groups. Small rural schools with relatively few staff may be able to train all school personnel at once. Large schools may want to conduct several trainings so that group size remains manageable.

Some schools schedule training at a special staff meeting before the school year begins. Others offer training on a regularly scheduled staff inservice day during the school year. Some even train teaching staff during their planning periods over a two-day period, and then allow them to leave school early on these days. Having conducted training in a variety of ways, we find that school staff least prefer after school training. Some staff report difficulties concentrating on the material at the end of the day, particularly if the day has been stressful. After school training also eliminates the possibility of certain staff attending (e.g., coaches, bus drivers).

Regardless of how training is scheduled, we recommend that the length of training be approximately an hour-and-a-half to two hours. Because school staff have a more prescribed role in assisting high-risk youth than crisis response team members, two hours should be sufficient to cover the requisite material.

Staff training may be provided by experts from the community or by members of the crisis response team. Regardless of who does the training, presenters should use a variety of methods to teach the material, including lecture, audiovisual materials, small group exercises, presentation of case studies, role play, and paper-and-pencil exercises (Ryerson, 1987a). Handouts to accompany the presented material should be prepared as well.

Some trainers prefer to show a film as part of the training. Any film used in training should be previewed to determine its suitability. Films which show methods of suicide, are overly dramatic, or which glorify the subject should be avoided. There are excellent films for staff training which are produced by the National Committee on Youth Suicide and the American Association of Suicidology. These training films emphasize warning signs and helpful intervention strategies for school staff and parents, and many come with a discussion guide and take-home booklets.

Content of Staff Training

There are a number of commercially available training materials appropriate for staff presentations. For example, Barrett (1987), the California State Department of Education (1987a), Poland (1989), Ruof, Harris, and Robbie (1987), and Ryerson and King (1986) all provide material helpful for planning a staff inservice on suicide intervention and prevention. Training for school staff in suicide prevention should include the following:

- national, state, and local statistics on youth suicide (5 minutes);

- an emphasis on the need for training and the staff's role in identification and referral of at-risk youth (10 minutes);

- factors contributing to the increase in youth suicide (10 minutes);

- myths and facts about suicide (10 minutes);

- dynamics of the suicidal crisis, especially the importance of hopelessness (5-10 minutes);

- warning signs and the characteristics of high-risk youth (20 - 25 minutes);

- appropriate and inappropriate responses if confronted with a suicidal student [e.g., do not leave student alone; do not promise confidentiality; do not minimize the problem; ask simple questions to assess the immediate danger level; listen without judging, reflect student's feelings; act hopeful and positive; show concern and caring; get immediate help] (20 - 25 minutes);

- roles and responsibilities of the crisis response team, referral procedures for accessing the team, what to expect following referral, and identification of available community resources if students contact staff members after school or on the weekends (10 - 15 minutes);

- clarification of confidentiality issues and duty to report (5 minutes);

- empowerment emphasizing that even one staff member can make a difference given the situational nature of suicide and the ambivalence of most students who consider self-destruction; case examples of successful interventions by school staff (10 - 15 minutes);

- question and answer period (10 minutes or longer as needed).

In addition to this training, it is critical that all staff have knowledge of the school's crisis response plan. Staff members will want to know their roles in its implementation. If the postvention plan is discussed at the suicide prevention inservice, it will take up a large portion of the time needed to train staff in essential identification and referral skills. Therefore, we suggest that the plan be reviewed at a regularly scheduled all-staff meeting so that it can receive the attention it deserves. Ample opportunity should be provided for clarification and discussion. All staff members should receive a written copy of the plan. Once each year, the plan should be reviewed and updated (if necessary) by administrators and members of the crisis response team.

After the staff is trained, a plan should be developed for providing annual booster sessions. In our experience, we have found administrators resistant to scheduling yearly staff booster sessions of the same length as the original training. As a result, we recommend that for subsequent presentations, trainers keep it short (30 minutes or less), highlight only the most important information (warning signs and referral procedures), and provide written handouts with additional key points for school personnel.

A plan should also be developed for providing suicide prevention training to new school staff. If staff turnover in a school is low, it might be most cost-effective to videotape the original staff presentation for new employees to review. If films, paper-and-pencil exercises, or handouts were part of the original training, these should also be made available to new staff. Another option for schools with only one or two new staff is to coordinate training with other schools in the community whose staff need to be trained.

EDUCATING PARENTS

It is important that parents be offered suicide prevention education, as well as be kept apprised of the school's efforts to combat the problem. A few parents may openly resist any presentation on student suicide. More likely, however, most simply will not have the time or inclination to attend the school's parent education programs. At the minimum, therefore, parents should be mailed written information outlining the school's program. Parents need to know that a crisis response team is available and that school staff have been trained to identify and refer at-risk students. Other related programs the school has employed to enhance student self-esteem or teach coping skills should be highlighted as well.

Parents also should be sent written information which does the following: (1) dispels misperceptions about student suicide; (2) tells them how to identify potential suicidal risk in their children; (3) provides information about helpful ways to respond if they think their child needs help; and (4) identifies school and community helping resources. Similar to teachers and school staff, parents benefit from learning identification and referral skills.

Schools vary in how they send information to parents. Some schools send materials through direct mail, others include information with students' report cards. Still others include information in school or district newsletters that are mailed to parents' homes. Our experience is that the least reliable method of getting information to parents is to send it home with the students.

In addition to sending written materials to parents, we recommend providing a yearly suicide prevention education workshop for parents and interested members of the community. Parent organizations such as the PTA often are receptive to sponsoring parent workshops on this topic.

Schools may choose to contract with an outside expert to provide the parent training, or assign the task to members of the crisis response team. Regardless of who does the training, it is important for both administrators and team members to be present at the workshop in order to answer questions. It may also be helpful to invite a representative from the community mental health agency or suicide prevention hotline to answer parents' questions about community services. The content of parent training should be similar to that provided to school staff, with an emphasis on identification of warning signs, finding help in the community, effective communication, and fostering in their children feelings of hope.

In addition to a parent workshop, we recommend that at least once each year, the school newsletter feature an article on suicide prevention (e.g., the work of the crisis response team, review of warning signs and referral information, the adoption of new prevention curricula which enhance students' skills). Also on a yearly basis, we recommend that a member of the crisis response team contact area newspapers to update them about school efforts in preventing maladaptive student behavior (e.g., violence, suicide, teen pregnancy, substance abuse). Media articles specific to suicide should include warning signs, appropriate ways to respond to at-risk students, and referral resources.

THE TEAM APPROACH RECONSIDERED

A comprehensive school-based suicide prevention program which includes crisis response teams, trained teaching and support staff, and informed parents can reduce student suicide rates. Preliminary evidence consistently suggests that having trained staff, parents, and students increases referrals and results in fewer suicide attempts and deaths.

In Allegan County, Michigan, for example, the occurrence of seven teenage suicides in a six month period during the 1986-87 school year resulted in all nine school districts in the county developing and training crisis response teams. Following team training, school staff were trained in identification and referral skills. Peer helping programs followed teacher training in five of the nine school districts, and a student curriculum on suicide prevention was taught to all peer helpers. Parents received information on suicide prevention through school newsletters and community newspaper articles.

During the ten years prior to this rash of deaths, the county averaged two suicides per year. Following the implementation of the above program, there have been only two adolescent suicides in nearly eight years. Both of the victims were 19 years old and not enrolled in school at the time of the suicide. Both of these suicides occurred in communities without peer helping programs.

While the number of student suicides decreased following program implementation, what increased dramatically was the number of students referred to crisis response teams and community agencies for risk assessment and crisis intervention. Team members in each district, as well as community professionals, also reported fewer suicide attempts as high-risk students began to be referred earlier in the suicidal risk continuum.

The message here is clear: schools can and do make a difference in reducing suicide and other forms of risk among students. Crisis response teams, staff training and parent education, in conjunction with peer helping programs and age-appropriate curricula, form the basis of effective response.

5
ASSESSING SUICIDE RISK

The assessment of suicide risk among students should serve three purposes. First, it should provide for a sound judgment as to whether a student is in immediate danger and in need of help. Second, it should generate valuable information if referral to mental health specialists is necessary. Third, the assessment should provide for a determination of risk which may pose no immediate threat of suicide, but which could escalate into a suicidal crisis if no intervention is provided.

As implied, risk assessment also should permit a judgment, when appropriate, that a student is at no discernible risk and therefore warrants no school intervention or outside referral. This means that risk assessments of suicide-proneness should not confuse the existence of personal problems with a student's inability to deal with those problems, except through suicide. The task of assessing suicide-proneness is therefore different from that of identifying potential crisis events in a student's life. While the divorce of one's parents, being physically or sexually abused, or the death of a family member may constitute crisis events for students, they do not automatically produce self-destructive behavior.

How then are educators to know the level of suicide risk facing students? We find that the scholarly literature on forecasting suicide risk in students is confusing and not always defensible in terms of sound measurement practices. Nevertheless, developing effective suicide risk assessments is so important that the American Association of Suicidology ranks it as one of the organization's highest priorities (Yufit, 1991). Without better tools of risk evaluation, it is unlikely that we will be able to meet the goal established by the U.S. Department of Health and Human Services of reducing the incidence of suicide at least 10% by the year 2000 (DHHS, 1989).

We believe that the selection of appropriate risk measures, careful data collection, and valid interpretation should form the basis of subsequent intervention plans in schools and agencies alike. Yet such a task is not easy. True, there are some psychometric screening procedures available to help determine if a person is at risk of suicide. Nearly all of these tools, however, are for trained clinicians. What educators need are effective procedures to assist them in knowing when to refer suicidal students to clinicians. Educators also need to be able to identify students whose problems are less pronounced and who can be helped by programs at school.

From our experience in determining suicide-proneness among students, we have found that interviews, when properly conducted by educators and other professionals, yield valuable screening, referral, and intervention data. Properly conducted interviews simultaneously take into account certain of the students' psychological states, behaviors, and social situations. Such interviews can also lead to placing troubled students in direct communication with a professional capable of marshaling resources on their behalf.   Because of the importance of these interviews, therefore, educators must proceed with caution.

THE NEED FOR CAUTION

It is impossible to predict youth suicide in every case. The best that anyone can hope to accomplish with an assessment tool for educators is to construct a reasonably accurate profile of suicide-proneness.   Such assessment is necessary to direct educators in making decisions about the character of services students may need.   To do this, the assessment tool must be derived from research. Fortunately, there is a basis for assessing student suicide risk in the work of scholars and clinicians.   However, caution is in order when using any assessment procedure.

One reason for caution is the problem of "false positives." A school can do great harm by inappropriately labeling students as being suicide-prone, when in fact they are not.   The danger here is more than simply misdirecting scarce resources.   The real danger is in labeling students in a fashion which calls inappropriate attention to them.   Such labels may even evoke a self-fulfilling prophecy which produces a crisis where before there was none.

Most students who are experiencing serious problems (e.g., pregnancy, substance abuse, low achievement) will not attempt self-destruction.   Suicide is a relatively rare event given the large number of students with problems, including those with very serious problems.   Enacting a suicide intervention plan should be reserved only for those cases where the data suggest a reasonable expectation that a student might take drastic action.   Obviously, no intervention plan should be enacted without first conducting a proper assessment of that risk.

There is another reason for caution. No suicide screening inventory which elicits information from students has gotten around a fundamental problem: the denial of suicidal thoughts and intentions when such thoughts and intentions are present. A small proportion of high risk students who are contemplating suicide will vehemently deny such intentions.

To minimize this problem, the screening must ensure as much validity and reliability as possible (i.e., the accuracy and the consistency of the information being gathered). The reliability of information can be determined by the consistency in student responses to a variety of probing questions. An estimate of the validity can be made by securing consistent but independent data from outside the interview (e.g., observations from teachers, parents, and peers). This means that it is important to check what students say in interviews against what others have seen or heard.

Whenever conducting a suicide assessment interview, feedback from other professionals should be sought following the assessment. At least two members of the crisis response team should review the data collected from student interviews. This builds greater confidence in interpretation. It also constitutes sound practice should questions of liability arise.

Although interviewers may want to seek additional feedback from teachers and from a student's peers as an independent check on data gathered from an interview, this poses a dilemma. On the one hand, by seeking independent information, the interviewer risks a possible breach of confidence. If the interviewer carelessly raises false alarms by inappropriately seeking more information, damage can be done to the student. On the other hand, additional information often is critical to an accurate determination of a student's suicidal potential, especially when a student denies suicidal intentions despite clear warning signs to the contrary.

Because the health and safety of a student is at stake, there are several rules of thumb to guide an interviewer in seeking additional information. Most often a student will have been referred to the interviewer because of reports from a teacher. For example, a teacher may have initiated a report based on personal observations or because of hear-say reports from a student's peers. In such cases, it is appropriate for the interviewer to approach the source of the report in order to confirm the information first hand. *It is not a breach of ethics to follow-up on a report by approaching the source of that report.* Doing so provides an opportunity not only to check on the information, but to caution others not to inappropriately share this information with those who do not need to know.

A more problematic situation arises when the interviewer wishes to approach a peer who is believed to have valuable information which has *not* been fully disclosed (e.g., they may have knowledge of their friend's suicide plans). If it is judged that a close associate (e.g., boyfriend, girlfriend, best friend) is in a position to supply critical health or safety information, it is acceptable to discreetly approach that friend. However, it is not acceptable for the interviewer to indicate that the need for seeking information is because it is thought that the student in question might be suicidal. Rather, the interviewer should stick to specifics such as the following: "There has been some concern expressed about the well-being of your friend. Is there anything that you can tell me which might help me to help him?"

The purpose of such questioning is to gently and discreetly probe in areas where the student's health and safety are believed to be jeopardized, without labeling the student suicidal or revealing confidential information. Close peers are usually in a position to provide new insights, especially if they believe that this information will truly help their friend. If there are any doubts as to whether the interviewer should approach peers for such questioning, it is helpful to seek the opinion of another school crisis team member.

In some instances, interviewers are well-advised to seek information from peers through indirect means. This is particularly true in cases where soliciting information would have the unintended consequence of generating rumors that crisis team members have targeted a student as suicidal. A better means of gathering such information might be to ask the referring school staff member to approach the peer and discreetly ask questions. School personnel, however, should first receive guidance as to the appropriate method of soliciting information.

This raises a final note of caution over possible liability. There are two broad areas related to risk assessment where schools can be held liable.

One area of potential liability is if the school has no crisis intervention plan in place. A growing number of schools are now mandated by law to establish plans for crisis intervention. To be effective, such plans necessitate a means of identifying those at high risk. This suggests possible charges of negligence if the school makes little or no effort to identify and help suicidal students. This is especially true if suicidal behaviors or statements were clearly present before a suicide. It therefore behooves schools to establish procedures for conducting assessments of suicide-proneness as part of a crisis intervention plan.

The other area of potential liability is concerned with *how* risk assessments are conducted. Risk assessment is serious business; it cannot be done in a casual manner. Despite good intentions, improper screening followed by inappropriate interventions can make a school doubly liable. Thus it is important that educators do not attempt to take actions beyond their sphere of competence or professional responsibility (e.g., providing "therapy" without authorization).

Educators cannot and should not be expected to conduct clinical diagnoses. That is the job of mental health professionals. Legally and ethically, however, educators are expected to *screen* students for the purpose of *referring* those determined to be at possible risk of suicide. We may summarize these liability concerns in a single sentence: "Schools are damned if they don't and damned if they do it badly."

THE INTERVIEW SCHEDULE

It may be difficult to communicate with a potentially suicidal student in an interview, especially if the interviewer is unknown to the student, or if the student is agitated, hostile, or suspicious of adults. What the interviewer says and does in the first few minutes will be critical in setting the tone. It is imperative for students to perceive their interviewer as caring, empathic, and helpful. One should, therefore, keep in mind several rules for effective communication.

Establish Rapport

- Speak slowly and calmly. The more in control and confident one appears, the more security it provides to the student.

- When responding to an adolescent, use basic terms such as sad, angry, hurt, scared, confused, and guilty. Avoid using technical or therapeutic jargon.

- Label and reflect the student's feelings by using phrases such as "It sounds as if you are feeling . . .;" "I'm hearing you say that you are . . .;" "I wonder if you are . . .;" "What you seem to be saying is that you are . . .;" and so forth.

- Refrain from minimizing a student's problems and never dismiss a student's thoughts or feelings as ridiculous or exaggerated. Comments such as "I'm sure you don't mean that," or "This is not a big deal," or "You are overreacting," serve to inhibit communication. Always encourage the honest expression of feelings.

- Do not act judgmental. Expressions of anger or irritation, or moralizing about the student's lack of responsibility, only makes that person feel more isolated and vulnerable. Remarks such as "You're being selfish," or "How could you do this to your parents," or "Life is tough — get on with it," are inappropriate.

- Resist the urge to begin problem solving during the initial part of the interview. Attempts to problem solve too early may result in students discounting, rejecting, or "yes butting" whatever is said. Listen attentively without interrupting and reflect their feelings; this will elicit open communication.

These suggestions are aimed at establishing good rapport with those in need of help. To further accomplish this, Klott (1988a) recommends using a three part procedure. First, state the reasons why a student is being seen (e.g., grades dropping, disinterest in pleasurable activities, substance abuse, acting-out, told someone about suicidal thoughts). Second, show concern. Third, invite the student to talk about his or her problems. Below are examples:

If You Don't Know the Student:

1. "_____ (teacher, parent, or peer who referred student) told me that you just haven't been yourself lately. Things seem pretty rough for you right now. They noticed that . . . (e.g., grades dropping, tired all the time, getting in trouble, looking sad)."

2. "They are worried about you and told me about it. What they said concerns me too. I'm worried about you. We all care about what happens to you."

3. "Is there something bothering you that we can talk about? What has been happening recently with you?"

If You Know the Student:

1. "You haven't been yourself lately. I have noticed . . . (e.g., grades dropping, getting in trouble, looking sad). (Cite factual rather than inferential data.)

2. "I'm very worried about you. I care what happens to you. I'd like to help."

3. "Is there something bothering you that we can talk about? Can we talk about what is happening?"

Some students will be unwilling or unable to verbalize their emotions. An interviewer can help by making statements that link experiences with "feeling words" (e.g., "When people experience what you've been going through, they often feel scared and confused.").

If a student refuses to communicate, let him or her know again that certain warning signs have been observed, that help is available, and that you are open to communicate. If the student still does not respond, he or she should be referred to another crisis team member who may be able to establish better rapport.

There are times when a student will appear to be at high risk for suicide, yet will refuse to communicate with any crisis team member. If this occurs, then a community mental health agency, hospital, or suicide prevention center should be contacted for guidance. Students who are hostile, noncommunicative, and who significantly resist efforts by the interviewer to establish rapport are at high risk. An unwillingness to form an alliance with a help-giving professional is frequently predictive of

noncompliance with future therapeutic recommendations
(Berman & Jobes, 1991).

ELICITING SUICIDE INFORMATION

Given the establishment of good rapport, the task for
school staff is then to elicit information which allows for
assessing the nature and level of a student's suicide
potential. This means coming to a determination about
whether the student is at high risk of suicide, where the
student should be referred, or whether the student does not
have sufficient problems to warrant special assistance.

To aid in assessment, we have identified seven
distinct but related areas which require data. This
information is especially useful if a referral is made to a
mental health agency or private therapist. It is also helpful
to those working with students who are referred to
in-school programs. These areas are:

- suicidal admissions;

- plans for committing suicide;

- behavioral history;

- social relationships;

- present motivations and thoughts relevant to
  suicide;

- perceptions of death; and

- plans for the future.

With these seven areas in mind, we have developed two suicide risk assessment tools. The first is an abbreviated version of the second. The abbreviated device can be used to conduct a preliminary screening of possibly high risk students. The second assessment tool — a focused interview protocol — is much more detailed and requires more time and training for proper use. This protocol could be used by school psychologists, school social workers, or other highly trained staff, as well as by mental health professionals with clinical expertise.

We have developed these suicide risk measures from a wide variety of available assessment materials, and from what the research literature indicates as being predictive of suicide. We have borrowed from and modified some of the ideas of those who have pioneered suicide risk assessment, adding our own ideas to those of others. Throughout, we have organized the measures in ways which reflect both common sense and prevailing expert opinion. The works of Barrett (1987), Berman and Jobes (1991), Capuzzi (1989), Davis and Sandoval (1991), Hafen and Frandsen (1986), Klott (1988a; 1988b), Maris, Berman, Maltsberger and Yufit (1992), Miller (1984), Pfeffer (1986), Steele (1992), Yufit (1989; 1991), and many others have helped us in this task.

Preliminary Suicide Screening in School

The identification of suicidal students increasingly is emerging as an expectation for those working in school settings. The majority of educators, however, lack training in clinical diagnosis. This is true for most mental health or related problems, including the assessment of suicide potential among students. To impose upon educators the expectation that they conduct clinical assessments would be unreasonable. It is reasonable, however, to expect those working in schools — especially those with training in counseling — to identify serious problems which impact on a student's health and safety, and then make referrals accordingly.

The task of identifying potentially suicidal students does not require educators to have clinical expertise. It does require that they be able to discern gross indicators which clinicians believe signal high suicide potential. To aid them in this task, use of a preliminary screening tool is in order. An effective screening tool should meet several requirements for use in educational settings. It should be simple to use, it should require only a brief amount of time to administer, and it should be accurate enough to identify the possibility of imminent suicide risk. When such risk is identified, a referral should be made to those professionally trained to conduct a more thorough clinical assessment.

From the preliminary screening tool, we have identified those items which are most closely associated with high suicide risk. The rationale for selecting these items is included in the complete protocol. Anyone using the abbreviated version should first examine the full array of questions and their rationale presented in the unabbreviated focused interview.

YOUTH SUICIDE
PRELIMINARY SCREENING

The preliminary screening tool should be used in schools or other settings where adults are in contact with students. The purpose is to identify young people who are at highest risk of self-destruction, and then to refer them to those who are professionally trained to conduct more complete assessments. *This tool should only be used to determine whether or not to make a referral. It should not serve as the only basis for clinical diagnosis and therapy.*

A referral immediately should be made to a trained clinician when a student responds to *any* question where the word "referral" appears in parentheses. These are unequivocal indicators of serious risk.

The other indicators *may* produce suicidal behavior, depending upon the intensity of each and its combination with other items. We have placed a "1" next to problematic responses, and have cautiously selected a score of *three or more* as a convenient (albeit arbitrary) point at which to make a referral for a more careful assessment.

1. Are you thinking seriously about harming yourself?

    ❑ No
    ❑ Yes (refer)

2. Do you have a plan for harming yourself?

    ❑ No
    ❑ Yes (refer)

3. If you have been considering suicide, do you have the means to take your own life (e.g., gun, pills)?

    ❑ No
    ❑ Yes (refer)

4.   Have you made a previous suicide attempt?

❑ No
❑ Yes (+1)

(If *yes:*)

a.   When? _____

b.   Do any adults who can help you know about this?

❑ Yes
❑ No (+1)

c.   Did you receive any help following your attempt?

❑ Yes
❑ No (+1)

d.   Do you still want to die?

❑ No
❑ Yes (refer)

5.   Have any of your family or close friends attempted suicide or taken their own lives?

❑ No
❑ Yes (+1)

6.   Are you having serious trouble at school, at home, or with the law?

❑ No
❑ Yes (+1)

7. Can you see any way to solve your problems?

    ❑ Yes
    ❑ No (+1)

8. Do you have anyone to turn to for help or support right now?

    ❑ Yes
    ❑ No (+1)

9. Do you get drunk or "high" on other drugs at least twice per week?

    ❑ No
    ❑ Yes (+1)

10. Do you feel deeply guilty or extremely angry about things that have happened?

    ❑ No
    ❑ Yes (+1)

11. Do you have any hope that the future will be better?

    ❑ Yes
    ❑ No (+1)

SCORE _____ (If three or more, conduct the following Focused Interview Protocol or refer to a mental health professional.

FOCUSED INTERVIEW PROTOCOL

The goal of conducting a more comprehensive assessment of suicide risk is to answer three basic questions:

1) accuracy — Is the person truly at risk?

2) magnitude — How great is the risk? Is the student in imminent danger?

3) source — What is the cause of the crisis?

From such determinations, appropriate interventions can be formulated. Unfortunately, a foolproof youth suicide assessment device has not been developed.

The American Association of Suicidology and many clinicians and scholars are working to improve the "art" of suicide prediction. Our bias in this regard is clear: we believe that the best way at this time to determine accuracy, magnitude, or source of suicide risk is through focused interviews. While the preliminary screening device is a useful place to start, only in-depth interviews can provide the level of information necessary. A trained school or community professional should conduct one or more focused interviews which revolve around the seven themes previously mentioned.

Suicidal Admissions

It is critical to assess the frequency, duration and intensity of a person's thoughts about death as a way of escaping pain. The more time and energy spent thinking about death, the higher the risk. If such thoughts are fleeting or infrequent, then the risk is lower. This is especially true if the student indicates that he or she tries to resist such thoughts. The following questions allow for determining the frequency, duration and intensity of thoughts about death.

1. Have you ever wanted to die? When?

2. How frequent are these thoughts?

3. How long have you had these thoughts?

4. How long do these thoughts last?

5. How do these thoughts make you feel (e.g., scared, hopeless, depressed, try to fight thoughts)?

The following questions should be asked directly. Furthermore, it is important that no comments or judgments be made after the student replies to them. One may begin by making empathic statements which reflect negative feelings expressed earlier (e.g., "You told me some things earlier that make me worried about you. You said ...., so I'm concerned about you. I'm wondering ..."

6. Have you been thinking about harming yourself in some way?

7. Have you been thinking about killing yourself?

8. How long have you been thinking about killing yourself?

9. How often do you think about killing yourself?

10. When are you most likely to think about it?

Most suicide-prone adolescents will respond honestly if asked questions in this manner. If a student says nothing about having suicidal thoughts but the interviewer has reason to suspect otherwise, it is better for the interviewer to be cautious and refer the student to another crisis team member. If both team members have reason to believe that the student is not being forthright, then it is wise to seek guidance from a mental health professional.

Of course, if a student admits to seriously considering suicide, then immediate referral to an appropriate mental health agency outside the school should occur. In addition, any special services provided for that student at school should be done only with guidance from mental health professionals.

Assessing the Suicide Plan

If a student feels hopeless and has a clear suicide plan, then the risk is greatest. For example, the more that a suicide plan is detailed, specific, and thought out, the greater the immediate danger. In such cases, referral to outside mental health professionals should be automatic.

Even if a student has only a vague plan, this does not mean that he or she is at low risk. Impulsive students may attempt suicide without much planning. This is particularly true for acting-out, hostile and aggressive adolescents.

There are two general rules which should guide the actions of those in contact with students in crisis. First, the more immediate the plan for self-destruction, the greater the risk level. For example, a student who plans on attempting suicide tomorrow is at much higher risk than one who has vague plans for next month. Second, the more lethal the plan, the greater the danger. Guns, hanging, and jumping are among the most lethal. Cutting or poisoning by gas or pills — while still lethal — take more time to result in death.

The proximity of possible rescuers is also important in weighing the danger. Planning to attempt suicide at 6:00 P.M. in a bedroom when parents are home is somewhat less risky than attempting suicide in an isolated area at 3:00 A.M. With these considerations in mind, the interviewer should first ask if there is a plan. If so, follow up with questions which attempt to ascertain the character of that plan. Therapists will find such information extremely valuable.

11. Do you have a plan for killing yourself?

12. Can you tell me about it?

13. How would you do it?

14. When did you plan to do this?

15. Where did you plan to do this?

16. Does anyone else know of this plan?

If a student responds to questions about a plan with any answer other than a clear "No," then the answer may be intended to divert the interviewer from the truth. If a student says such things as "None of your business," or "I'd rather not say . . . it's too embarrassing," or "It's not that serious," then these may tentatively be viewed as "Yes" responses which require further probing.

If the student admits to having a suicide plan, but refuses to talk about it, then he or she is probably in extreme danger. This could mean that the student does not want to be talked out of attempting suicide.

If a plan is expressed, then it is helpful to know the lethality of the method *from the student's perspective.* Even if the method is to make a superficial cut on the wrist or to consume a small handful of aspirin, if the student *believes* this will result in death, the risk of suicide is great.

>   17.   Do you think that _____ (the method chosen) will kill you?

Lethality also is higher if there is a readily available means to commit suicide. For example, having easy access to a loaded gun is more dangerous than having to buy or steal one.

>   18.   Do you have the gun (pills, rope, knife) now?
>   19.   Is the gun (pills, rope, knife) in the house or do you have to get it (them)?
>   20.   Is the gun loaded or unloaded?
>   21.   Is the gun (medicine) locked up?
>   22.   Do you have a key?

In cases where students have a clear suicide plan, it is important for them to think about alternatives, even before mental health professionals see them. By asking questions such as "What would have to happen to make you *not* consider hurting yourself?," the interviewer may discover that a seemingly insignificant future event will help change a student's mind about dying. This is also a first step in identifying the conditions necessary to reestablish in these students a sense of hope.

Examining Behavioral History

If a student previously attempted suicide, and plans to attempt again, he or she is at the highest level of risk. The more recent and the more serious the previous attempt, the greater the immediate danger. Gathering this information, as well as the student's impression of the lethality level of the past attempt, will prove to be of great value to therapists receiving the referral.

23. Have you ever made a previous suicide attempt? When?

24. Did you think that _____ (method chosen) would kill you?

If a previous attempt was made, the interviewer should find out if any intervention was provided. If the attempt was ignored by significant others and no help was given, the present risk level is very high. Equally important, if the events that triggered the past attempt are still unresolved, then the risk level also remains high.

25. Following your last attempt, were you hospitalized?

26. Did you receive therapy in a place other than a hospital? For how long?

27. What was going on in your life then?

28. Are the same things going on now?

If the student expresses hope or thankfulness about still being alive, then the risk is less. Also, if the youth expresses remorse over the attempt, then the risk level is lower than if no remorse is expressed. But if he or she expresses anger or frustration about being rescued or having failed the attempt, then the danger level remains very high.

29. How do you feel about still being alive?

30. Do you regret having attempted to take your own life?

31. How do you feel about having been rescued?

Because a significant percentage (possibly as many as twenty-five percent) of those who complete suicide have had a previous suicide in the family, the next questions are very important. The closer a student's emotional ties to the person who committed suicide, the greater the immediate risk if that student appears to be coping poorly. The same applies if a close friend completed suicide. This is an especially risky time if those close to the student frequently talk about suicide as a valid way of coping with pain. Again, such information is very helpful to therapists who receive referrals of suicide-prone students.

32. Do any of your family or close friends talk about committing suicide?

33. Did any of your family or close friends attempt suicide or take their lives?

34. How old were you when it happened?

35. What was your relationship with that person?

Assessing Social Relationships

States of depression, anger, guilt, and estrangement in the context of hopelessness are consistently associated with suicidal students. We know that if students who face serious problems feel isolated, rejected, or cut-off from significant others, they are at high risk of developing a depressed condition which could provoke suicide. Some are also likely to feel a deep anger which they may direct toward others or which they turn inward. This is particularly true in cases where there is serious family dysfunction (e.g., substance abuse, bitter divorce, neglect, physical or sexual abuse). In such cases, it is important to see how the student characterizes the nature of the abuse or other dysfunction. Again, this provides important background information for referrals both within and outside the school.

36. Does anyone in your family regularly use too much alcohol or drugs?

37. How do you get along with your parents right now? Your brothers and sisters?

38. How were you treated growing up in your parents' house? Were you or anyone else in your family ever abused?

If a student characterizes the immediate family in ways which are clearly dysfunctional, then it is important to explore other potential sources of support. A student who states "No one is there for me," often will go on to give examples of persons who were supportive in the past and who are still potentially available for nurturance.

39. How do you get along with other family members (i.e., grandparents, aunts, uncles)?

40. Do you have any close friends?

41. Are there any teachers or other people at school whom you are close to?

42. Do you have a girlfriend (boyfriend) right now?

In exploring these relationships, remember that the amount and the quality of communication between the student and his or her significant others is important. Often the student has not discussed his or her feelings with anyone. Very likely the student has honestly tried to communicate, but has received responses from others that are defensive, denying, rejecting, angry, or punishing. Perhaps the youth has tried to communicate in such an angry, manipulative, or blaming way that others did not respond with understanding or support. The end result is that the student may feel "disconnected" from others. For highly depressed or angry youth, where communication appears to have completely broken down between family or close friends, and the student expresses little sense that others care, referral to mental health experts is prudent.

43. Have you talked to anyone else about how you feel? Who? When?

44. Did they listen and were they helpful to you?

45. Do you have anyone you can turn to for support right now?

46. Who are the persons you are closest to and how involved are they with you right now?

47. Who is the person you most trust?

The more hopeless a student feels about getting relief from pain, the higher the risk, especially if there was a previous suicide attempt. Without successful intervention, chances increase that the student will again act on his or her suicidal thoughts. If the student was helped before and is willing to seek help again, he or she is at lower risk. If the young person received professional help but found it aversive, and now shows no interest in obtaining this kind of help again, then he or she is at higher risk. Once again, troubled students who appear suicidal, yet who refuse to accept help, should be referred to a mental health specialist.

48. Are you now seeing (or have you seen) a counselor?

49. Did it help (or is it helping)?

50. What did you like (or not like) about seeing a helper?

51. How do you feel about accepting help from adults?

Assessing Suicide Motivations

A student's anger at others is an important motivating force in his or her contemplation of suicide. In general, the angrier the student, the more dramatic and shocking the method of attempting suicide might be. It is therefore important to assess this anger and to identify some of the adolescent's motives for considering suicide. Such motives may include wanting to: (a) gain attention; (b) receive help or get needs met; (c) manipulate others; (d) escape from an intolerable situation; (e) punish or get revenge on others. Obtaining this information can result in helping the student redefine the problem so as to seek help rather than consider suicide.

52. Who do you think would care the most if you took your life?

53. How do you think — (parents, friends, girlfriend, boyfriend, teachers) would feel if you took your life?

54. What do you hope will happen if you die?

If the student is terminally ill, suicide may be a way to control when death will occur. Even if the student is not seriously ill, many of those who complete suicide have been to see a physician in the six months before their death because of somatic complaints (i.e., stomachaches, headaches, muscular tension). This can be a warning sign.

55. Have you seen a doctor in the last six months? If so, for what?

Some students, particularly young adolescents, may want to commit suicide so they can be reunited with a loved one who has recently died.

56. Has someone you've been close to died recently?

57. Has this person's death made you want to die in order to be with him or her?

Students who are in serious trouble at school, at home, or with the law can become suicidal in anticipation of expected punishment (Brent et al. 1993). They can be motivated to consider suicide as a way to avoid the punishment, embarrassment, or humiliation they feel certain is forthcoming.

58. Have you recently been in trouble at school, at home, or with the law?

Perfectionistic, high-achieving and driven students who fear failure can also be at risk. Their self-worth is linked to their achievement. They may believe that failure means an intolerable loss of love, or loss of approval and validation from others. This perceived failure can precipitate a suicidal crisis. In addition, the interviewer may discover that some learning disabled or low achieving students whose parents hold unrealistically high expectations for them also are at higher risk for suicide (depending upon their responses to previous questions). The following questions tap these issues.

59. How are you doing in school right now?

60. Do you feel a lot of pressure to do well? From whom?

61. What do you think would happen if you didn't do as well as you would like?

There are some students who are filled with guilt, self-blame and self-hatred. Often they are the victims of prolonged physical or sexual abuse, rape victims, or possibly those who are suffering from a crisis of sexual identity. They may be motivated to consider suicide as a way to be punished for their imagined wrongdoings or failures.

62. Do you often feel guilty about things that happened to you?

63. Do you blame yourself when things go wrong?

64. Do you feel that you are a bad person? Why?

It is worth noting that no single response to the above questions is sufficient to warrant the conclusion that a student is going to commit suicide. Rather, the *pattern* of responses, in conjunction with other information gathered, should help the interviewer make a judgment as to whether the student can be helped by the school or should be referred elsewhere.

Perceptions of Death

Seriously depressed, guilty, angry or estranged students who hold immature or unrealistic views of death (e.g., they see death as comforting or romantic) are at high risk. Possibly they fail to see death as final, or they may envision death as a mystical state from which they can magically return. Asking if they see themselves at their own funeral is often a good way to get information about their views of death. Asking them who they see at their funeral and how they feel about what they see also provides insight into their motivations for attempting suicide (e.g., "They're all crying. I'll bet they're all sorry now for the way they treated me. I hope they feel really bad.''). Once again, this constitutes important background information for those receiving a referral.

65. What do you expect death to be like?
66. Do you see yourself at your own funeral? What do you see? How does that make you feel?

Determining Future Orientation

We have argued that hopelessness in the face of an intolerable situation is a basic element in youth suicide. On the other hand, hope that the future will be better is a deterrent to suicide. Suicidal students have a limited future time orientation; often they appear to be stuck in the past or focused only on their immediate problems. But when students are making plans for tomorrow, it is a sign of hope. It is therefore important to determine how the student sees the future and if he or she has appropriate plans.

67. What has been keeping you alive so far?
68. Do you have any plans for next week? Next year?
69. Do you have any hope that the future will be better?
70. Do you see your problems as temporary or permanent?
71. Can you see any way to solve your problems?
72. Do you get drunk or "high" to escape your problems? How often?

If a troubled student indicates that he or she copes by regularly getting high or drunk, by running away, or by engaging in risk-taking with friends, then the student needs help, even if he or she is not presently considering suicide. Without help, such problems could escalate into a suicidal crisis.   At the very least, such behaviors impair the student's competencies.   If the student's answers reflect adaptive behaviors (e.g., "I talk with friends about how I feel;" or "I stay busy;" or "I play sports"), then the risk is lower.   The risk is also less immediate if there are significant events (e.g., graduation, birthday, prom)   or significant persons (e.g., mother, boyfriend) that positively orient the student to the future.

Remember that hopelessness about the future, expressed through deep and prolonged depression, guilt, anger or estrangement, is extremely dangerous.   If such students perceive themselves as helpless, and their situation as hopeless with no way out, then they are at very high risk and should be referred to a mental health professional.

Throughout the questioning, interviewers should observe the match between the level of emotion expressed and the severity of the problem(s) presented.   A poor match shows one of two problems.   If the student presents a terrible situation with little or no emotion, then this can indicate a dangerous level of risk.   If the student expresses greater emotional intensity than seems appropriate in light of his or her problems, then the precipitating event may only be the latest in a series of losses or stressors in the student's life.   This too can be dangerous.   Unresolved past emotional traumas may be fueling the present crisis, thus keeping the student in an agitated and hopeless state.

Conclusion

This focused interview should generate sufficient information to identify those students at highest risk for suicide. In using this information, mental health specialists, school counselors, and crisis team members should collaborate to determine school responses in the following areas:

- the nature and extent of school interventions for students in need of help;

- the school's ability to deliver appropriate interventions for students at various levels of risk;

- the legal and ethical consequences following any assessment decision.

Remember that the preliminary screening instrument and the focused interview schedule are tools for making judgments about students. They can be used in conjunction with other measures appropriate for clinical settings. The information gathered should serve to guide decisions about how best to help.

Any helping action the school undertakes should be within its capabilities to deliver. Schools cannot and should not attempt to supplant the functions of community mental health organizations. Rather, in cases where a student is believed to be suicidal, school actions should be an adjunct to the actions of those agencies or private therapists receiving the school's referrals. In areas where school-based interventions are appropriate, educators should use the assessment information to develop effective ways of improving the competencies of their students.

6
CRISIS INTERVENTION

$\mathbf{R}$ecognition of a problem through risk assessment is only a first step in crisis intervention. Following assessment, activities must be directed toward students in need in order to reduce their immediate danger, and in the long term, place them on a path which will lead to recovery.

For those judged to be suicidal, diminishing immediate danger includes removing lethal means of self-destruction, mental health counseling, careful monitoring of behavior, and when possible, altering stressful aspects of the student's environment. In cases where the student is chemically dependent, reducing immediate danger also requires treatment for substance abuse as a first priority. Suicidal young people who are substance abusers will continue to experience distorted perceptions, emotional confusion, and feelings of hopelessness so long as the abuse persists. No attempts at long term intervention will be successful until they are drug free.

In the long term, however, at least two other tasks are needed in order to help troubled students. First, potentially suicidal students must be taught basic coping skills.

Confusion, low self-esteem, pain and hopelessness are reduced by fostering in young people the ability to solve problems. Second, the help of parents should be enlisted in order for intervention plans to succeed. Accomplishing these two tasks — teaching students problem solving skills and securing parental cooperation — are at the heart of effective crisis intervention in schools.

Effective crisis intervention also means that school staff cannot and should not act alone in working with students assessed to be at high risk of suicide. Collaboration with mental health professionals is essential. Nevertheless, educators can play an important role in teaching all students, including those judged to be at high risk of suicide, how to solve problems. Most mental health professionals and educators agree on this key point: basic problem solving instruction is helpful to all students, but it is especially helpful in preventing troubled youth from acting on suicidal impulses.

If students develop an arsenal of coping skills, then they are likely to feel balance and control when facing problems. In turn, this sense of control diminishes feelings of hopelessness. But how are educators to help students develop such an arsenal?

FOSTERING PROBLEM SOLVING SKILLS

Students experiencing profound hopelessness which could lead to suicide need to gain a sense of equilibrium. They also need help obtaining the resources to solve problems for themselves. The reasoning here is simple: educators cannot solve most problems for students. Therefore the task for educators is to foster in students the coping skills which will allow them to solve their problems in ways which are acceptable.

Most students at *low* risk of suicide can be engaged in the problem solving process if they have good rapport with school staff. Frequently these students develop adaptive solutions to problems with minimal direction. Simply discussing the problem helps them to see alternatives. With guidance, they are able to understand the steps necessary to circumvent problems and to reach new goals. Striving to achieve goals is a palliative against feelings of hopelessness.

For students at *high* risk of suicide, the task is more difficult. An overwhelming sense of hopelessness undermines their ability to generate nonsuicidal alternatives. The "solutions" they do generate are often unrealistic or unachievable. These students are pessimistic that anything will be effective in ameliorating their problems. Because they feel powerless, it is a challenge to help them realize their own abilities to create a hopeful future.

Helping high suicide risk students often requires more resources than is possible to give in the school setting. These students will need a continuing therapeutic relationship with a mental health professional. Yet most students, including those judged to be at potential risk of suicide, can learn problem solving skills with the aid of a school counselor, teacher, or other staff member. In other words, the school has a role to play in teaching all students — especially those with academically and personally debilitating problems — more effective ways to cope.

Teaching students in crisis how to solve problems is best accomplished in a systematic, step-by-step fashion.

We have delineated six steps in this process.   These steps are:

1.   Clarify the Problem

2.   Establish Appropriate Goal

3.   Brainstorm Alternatives for Reaching Goal

4.   Evaluate and Select Alternatives

5.   Specify Steps to Implement Plan

6.   Evaluate Effectiveness of Plan

Clarify the Problem

Many students with debilitating problems, especially those whose problems compel them to feel hopeless, will describe these problems in vague and global ways. For example, they may have difficulty in recognizing the specific experiences (e.g., death, divorce, peer rejection, academic failure) causing their pain. Their discussion instead may focus on what they perceive as their personal inadequacies (e.g., "I'm a loser;" "I never do anything right"), or on some vague external locus of control (e.g., "Everyone tries to get me.").

In such cases, the goal of problem clarification is clear: move the focus away from these negative global attributions toward a definition of the problem which allows for concrete resolution (Klott, 1988a). To do this, an important starting point is to focus on recent losses or rejections that may be contributing to the present crisis. A trained professional can help the student identify these specific events by using listening techniques such as paraphrasing, clarifying, summarizing, and asking open-ended questions. These techniques are illustrated as follows:

Paraphrasing: "What I hear you saying is . . ."

Clarifying: "I'm unclear about what you said. Do you mean that . . . ? Are you saying that . . . ?"

Summarizing: "I hear you saying several things. The important points you're making seem to be . . ."

Questioning: "When did it happen? How long has this been going on? How did that make you feel? Could you tell me more about that?"

Because troubled students often have a history of painful experiences, it is helpful to focus problem solving efforts on one small but manageable area at a time. Often this means focusing attention on the latest precipitating event in order to help the student gain a sense of control. It is important to ask what has happened recently to make the student feel this way. Simply talking about the problem may reduce confusion and suicidal impulses. Asking the following questions will help:

• What has happened recently to make you feel so depressed (or hopeless)?

• Which event(s) in the past made you most upset? When did this happen? Does this still upset you?

If the student discusses multiple problems (e.g., alcoholic parent, fights with peers, no friends, academic failure), it is important to summarize all the conflicts mentioned. Then have the student rank them by asking the following questions:

- Which of the problems you've mentioned are the most important to you?

- Which problems upset you the most?

- Which situation would you like to work on first?

Establish Appropriate Goal

Once the problem is clear, it is important to help the student develop a new and attainable goal. Obviously, this goal must not include harmful behaviors (e.g., getting drunk) that in turn increase the risk of suicide. This is no easy task, especially if the student is seriously contemplating suicide. These students often define their goals in narrow and unrealistic ways. Many troubled adolescents think in strictly dichotomous or "black and white" terms. Taken to the extreme, such thinking allows for only two options: death, or a magical solution.

Some students will hold unachievable goals which demand changing something over which they have no control. Trying to stop an alcoholic parent from drinking, or reuniting divorced parents, are common examples. Many hope to somehow magically change the past (e.g., making the team after tryouts are over; getting a girlfriend/boyfriend back after a breakup). Others set goals that have an all or none quality (e.g., being popular with everyone; getting all A's on a report card). Holding unrealistic goals, or hoping for magical solutions to problems, are invitations to failure.

If students in crisis define their most important goals in unattainable ways, then it is critical to help them redefine those goals. In order to guide students through this process, the school professional should do two things. First, try to identify each student's most important unmet needs. For example, a student who has experienced a broken romantic relationship will continue to have a need for companionship. Yet that student can be guided toward other means of securing companionship without expecting the former partner to return.

Second, in helping students in crisis to select a new goal, it is important to "start small" if possible. Setting reachable goals contributes to the adolescent's sense of accomplishment, empowerment, self-esteem and control. In order to avoid confusion, it is best to start with one manageable goal for each problem. The process of identifying needs and establishing new goals can begin with the following questions.

- How would you like to see the problem resolved? Is this realistic? Could it truly happen?

- What do you need to feel better now?

- What would you like to see happen?

- If _____ (unrealistic goal) can't happen, what else do you think would help you to feel better?

- What would have to happen (or not happen) to make you feel as if you reached your goal?

- What are some concrete things that could help you to feel you attained your goal?

It is important for the new goal to be specific. If the student states a goal in general terms (e.g., being popular, being happier, being more independent from parents, getting good grades), it is important to translate that goal into concrete behaviors that can be observed and measured. Oftentimes negotiating a "performance contract" with the student will help to create specific goals within a realistic timetable.

Brainstorm Alternatives for Reaching Goal

After the student has established a new goal, brainstorm with him or her alternative ways of reaching that goal. The idea is to create a sense that there are options. To facilitate this process, ask how the student has responded to disappointment, frustration, depression and anger in the past. This allows for a determination of the student's strengths and limitations in handling stress. The following questions are useful in directing this process.

- When you felt this way before, what did you do to make yourself feel better? Did it work? Would it help now?

- If it didn't work, what other things have helped you get through these feelings in the past?

It is important to acknowledge and reinforce any appropriate coping strategies the student has used in the past. In these cases, the student should be reassured with statements such as, "It sounds as if you coped well when that happened. As I see it, you handled a difficult situation in a positive way."

After examining past problem solving methods with the student, continue to explore additional alternatives. During the brainstorming process, the school professional should write down all the student's ideas without evaluating their practicality or effectiveness. The reason for this is that criticism of ideas during this phase will negatively affect the number and creativeness of solutions generated. Also, the student should be encouraged to generate more than one or two alternatives. The more ideas, the better the chance of producing a workable solution. It is important to direct the student with questions such as the following.

- How many possible ways can you think of to reach your goal?

- What are some of the things you've thought of doing?

- Are there other approaches you might consider to reach your goal?

Remember that many students, particularly those at highest risk, will need considerable direction in order to generate alternative ideas. The higher the level of suicide risk, the more that direction is necessary.

Evaluate and Select Alternatives

After several alternatives are generated, it is important to help the student assess the possible negative and positive consequences of each. In essence, this is a process of assessing the probabilities that each approach will produce the desired outcome in light of the student's circumstances and resources.

- What might happen if you do that? Will it happen right away or later?

- Is what you have suggested realistic?

- What are the chances that this approach will help you to reach your goal?

- What will other people (parents, teachers, peers) think and do if you do this?

- What are the costs and benefits of attempting this approach to solving the problem? Is there a better alternative?

Some students may continue to consider self destruction as an option. If this occurs, explore with them the negative consequences of suicide as a "solution" (e.g., permanence of death, aftermath for survivors). If this fails to dissuade the student, he or she should be referred to a mental health specialist.

After considering every option, allow the student to select the alternative(s) that best fits his or her needs and circumstances. Often alternatives will be combined and modified during this selection.

Specify Steps to Implement Plan

Once a plan is selected, it is critical to discuss the details of implementing that plan. This means considering in practical terms the concrete, sequential steps necessary to make the plan work. It is important to help the student decide upon a realistic timetable for starting and completing the plan. It is also important to identify any persons who might provide valuable support, and those who might create roadblocks. Attention to details at this stage can make the difference between a plan that works and one that does not. The following questions will help the student to clarify the steps involved.

- Let's write down all the steps you need to take in order to make the plan work. What has to happen first? What is the next thing you must do? Then what?

- Let's look at each step and ask "who, where, when, and how?"

- Who might help you in carrying out this plan?

- When will you start and how long do you think it will take?

The student and the school professional should consider contingencies if the plan fails or if circumstances prevent it from being carried out in full. Anticipating possible setbacks is especially important for potentially suicidal students. When there are setbacks, the student is less likely to behave dysfunctionally if a back-up plan is in place. Part of the contingency plan should be for the student to get in touch with the school professional as quickly as possible to rethink options if there is a setback.

- Let's think about what we can do if the plan doesn't work or if something unexpected happens. How will I know if that happens? Will you come to see me or call me so we can continue to work together?

Evaluate Effectiveness of Plan

As the last step in problem solving, the student and school professional should agree to get together again and evaluate the effectiveness of the plan. Depending on the plan, this may be the same day, the next day, or in a week. If part or all of the plan is not working, the student should be helped through the problem solving steps again. Even if the plan is working, however, several regularly scheduled follow-up sessions should occur. Such follow-up allows the school professional to reassess the student's suicide-proneness and to monitor the student's ability to enact coping strategies.

- When will we get back together to see if the plan is working?

As an adjunct to developing and evaluating problem solving plans, school professionals also should help students to identify and manage stressful situations. Students experiencing an immediate personal crisis, especially those at high risk of suicide, will require special help in managing their stress.

Stress Management

Both Barrett (1985) and Rotheram (1987) recommend helping adolescents identify stressful situations where the suicidal impulse is strongest, and then develop a plan for coping during these high risk times. Stress management, they feel, is critical to successful interventions with youth at risk.

Rotheram suggests helping students construct a "Feeling Thermometer" which describes feelings as units on a thermometer (from 0-100), with the student listing ten situations that are associated with different temperatures. Events which result in intense feelings of anger, stress, or depression receive higher numbers on the scale. The top of the scale represents to the student situations with an increased risk of provoking suicide. These may include family fights, death of a family member, rejection by significant others, or other troubling events.

After the Feeling Thermometer is constructed, students are helped to develop realistic plans for handling themselves in "hot" situations on their thermometer. These may include getting help from a trusted adult, talking to a supportive person, engaging in rigorous physical exercise, relaxing by taking deep controlled breaths and visualizing a peaceful scene, or consciously replacing negative thoughts with more positive ones (e.g., "I can't take this another moment — I have to kill myself" TO "This makes me very angry, but I'm not going to hurt myself because of it. Instead, I will . . ."). Some students may need to write their plan and carry it with them wherever they go.

This technique teaches students impulse control when it is most critically needed. It also helps them to differentiate their emotional states and to realistically assess the intensity of their feelings (Rotheram, 1987).

Both problem solving and stress management techniques are important elements in helping students overcome a suicidal or other crisis. Many experts suggest one additional step to help prevent high-risk students from engaging in self-destruction. Specifically, the use of a

"No-Suicide Contract" may make the difference in whether a student decides to live or die.

No-Suicide Contracts

Problem solving and stress reduction efforts with a troubled student will not always produce immediate success. In the midst of a serious crisis, some students do not have the capacity to meaningfully engage in such a process. However, potentially suicidal students may adhere to a written promise to abstain from suicidal behavior.

The use of a no-suicide contract allows high-risk students to recognize that although they may have suicidal thoughts, they need not act on them. This differentiation between thought and action is important. Ruof et al. (1987) found that many students who thought seriously about suicide felt they had no choice but to act on their ideation. Contracting can provide one barrier — perhaps the only barrier for some — between cognition and behavior.

The premise of a no-suicide contract is simple: the student, in the presence of a crisis team member or other school professional, agrees not to engage in any self-destructive behavior before first talking to that professional. In addition, the contract specifies what the student agrees to do if the professional cannot be immediately reached when the suicidal impulse is the strongest. The contract may also suggest what to do with available lethal methods.

After the specifics of the contract have been worked out, it should be written or typed in the presence of the student and signed by both the student and school professional. A copy of the contract should be given to the student.

Sample No-Suicide Contract*

I, _____ (name), agree not to take my own life or cause any harm to myself before first talking to _____ (school professional). If I begin feeling suicidal, I will call _____ (school professional) immediately at _____ (phone number).

If I cannot reach _____ (school professional), I will call _____ (another trusted adult) at _____ (phone). If I cannot reach _____ (school professional) or _____ (trusted adult), I will not harm myself before I can talk to one of them.

I also agree to immediately get rid of _____ (lethal method) which I could use to hurt myself.

Signed: _____

Date: _____

Witnessed By: _____

---
*Adapted from Getz, Allen, Myers, & Lindner, 1983.

Contracts are not appropriate to use with all adolescents, nor are they a substitute for therapy. Both Barrett (1985) and Smith (1988) caution against using contracts with persons who have violently shifting moods and loyalties. Included in this group are those addicted to alcohol or other drugs, and those diagnosed as manic-depressive, psychotic, or borderline personality disorder. We also agree with Barrett (1985) and Poland (1989) that a no-suicide contract should never be used alone, but only with such protective measures as parent contact, rallying external resources, and ensuring the physical safety of the adolescent (e.g., never leaving a suicidal student alone).

Some students at very high risk will refuse to sign a no-suicide contract. They refuse the contract because they do not want anyone interfering with their decision to die. These students require **immediate** help from mental health services in the community. Often they require hospitalization. These students should **not be left alone** for even a moment until they are placed in the protective custody of their parents or other adults who agree not to leave them unsupervised until outside help is available.

Consultation with Colleagues

After engaging the student in problem solving and stress reduction techniques, and after contracting, one important step remains. The school professional should consult with at least one other member of the crisis response team. This can be done in person or via the telephone if team members are unavailable. Peer consultation allows the professional to share the burden of decision-making. Working with suicidal youth is stressful; collaboration enhances a sense of support and creates a sounding board for developing ideas about how best to proceed. Colleagues may see things that were overlooked; meeting with them provides a forum for collaborative problem solving, for consensus building, and for reducing the liability of any single person. Equally important, consultation with colleagues reinforces a simple but vitally important fact: there can be many creative ways to intervene in a crisis.

School professionals may also wish to consult with a community mental health professional. Such consultation is especially valuable if the crisis team is unsure of the best way to intervene. It is prudent, however, to consult without revealing the student's name, although the pupil's responses to particular questions can be shared (Rouf et al. 1987). The community professional can then offer a judgment as to the most appropriate course of action for crisis team members to follow.

If the principal is not part of the crisis team, he or she should be asked to attend the crisis meeting. This allows the principal to be kept apprised of the intervention plan, including contact with parents. In cases where parents fail to obtain needed services for their child, the principal can assist in securing help.

Finally, although they sometimes are part of the problem, a student's parents are also part of the solution. The school is legally and ethically bound to contact the parents of a student suffering from a health or safety emergency. This includes the case of a suicidal student. Educators are wise, therefore, to develop creative strategies in which they can collaborate with parents in order to effectively help troubled students. Working with parents should be a critical part of the school's crisis intervention efforts.

7
WORKING WITH PARENTS

Many students experiencing a crisis are afraid when told that their parents will be contacted by school personnel. This may be especially true when a student is contemplating suicide. These students often anticipate (and sometimes rightly so) parental anger, denial, or punishment. For school personnel working with these students, it is necessary to acknowledge this fear. But it is equally necessary, on both ethical and legal grounds, to inform the parents of a health or safety emergency affecting their child. This is best done in the context of a face-to-face meeting.

The school professional should unequivocally state to the student that there is no choice but to contact parents when the risk of suicide is present. Explain that such contact is a professional and ethical obligation, particularly if a problem is life-threatening. Also explain the legal liability which could occur for not disclosing this information. Finally, explain that it is out of deep concern for the student's well-being that such information must not be kept secret.

After explaining the limits of confidentiality, spend time reflecting the student's feelings about this required breach. Some students may verbalize feelings of fear, anger, and betrayal; others will express relief that their plight is now being brought into the open. Listen and reflect their feelings. Empathic responding will go a long way toward helping them accept the need for parent contact. In addition, prepare students by explaining which information will be shared with their parents.

Many students will imagine a worse case scenario. In order to counteract this, it may help to ask the following questions:

- What is the worst that can happen when your parents find out?

- Is this likely to occur?

- If this happens, what can we do?

- What else might happen?

- What do you think is most likely to happen?

Another approach is to give students as much control as possible over how the parent contact will occur. Begin by asking some of the following questions:

- Would you like to call your parents and talk to them first while I stay in the room with you?

- If yes, what do you want to say and what would you prefer I say?

- Would you prefer if I call them?

- If they want to speak with you, will you speak with them on the phone, or would you like me to

tell them that you would rather talk to them when
they get here?

- When your parents come to school, what do you
  want to tell them and what do you prefer I tell
  them?

- Are there any other adults or family members who
  have been supportive of you that you would like to
  be at the meeting?

After the student has made some decisions, take a few
minutes to rehearse what he or she wants to say to one or
both parents. By providing both prompts and praise, the
student should feel more prepared to face what is to come.
The school professional will want to see the parents in
private for part or all of the first interview. Let the student
know this in advance. The goal throughout is to help the
student gain control and perspective. Empowering
adolescents in these ways can make a difference in their
response to further interventions and their receptiveness to
follow-up contacts.

Contacting Parents

How can school personnel notify parents in a way that
elicits support and cooperation rather than anger or denial?
Several guidelines are helpful. First, parents should be
contacted by the crisis team member who did the
assessment rather than a school administrator (unless the
administrator did the assessment). This is important
because the team member who saw the student has first
hand information which will corroborate the school's
concerns. In addition, crisis response team members have
made it their responsibility to be knowledgeable about

suicide assessment and crisis intervention. Their specialized knowledge can be shared with the parents, and their unique role communicates to the parents the seriousness of the risk.

Contacting parents can be stressful for the school professional, particularly if the parents respond in a hostile manner. For this reason, we concur with other experts (Ruof et al. 1987; Poland, 1989; Poland & Pitcher, 1990) that another team member, preferably an administrator, be on an extension during the phone interview to document the contact.

Ask parents to come to school for a face-to-face interview. If possible, another crisis team member should be present when parents arrive at the school for the conference. This initial parent interview should be conducted without the child being present. Someone should remain with the student during the parent interview. Ideally, both parents should attend the meeting. In cases of divorce, an attempt should be made to notify both parents, and at least the custodial parent should be asked to attend. If there is joint custody, both parents should be invited.

If Parents Cannot Be Reached

If parents cannot be reached during a health or safety emergency, the school must take responsibility for seeking necessary community services for the student. Threatened or attempted suicide constitutes such an emergency. It is therefore imperative to keep the child physically safe until parents can be notified. This may entail staying after school with the student until the parent arrives, or driving the pupil to a community mental health agency, suicide prevention center or hospital for emergency services. Just as school personnel have the right to seek emergency medical treatment for students in cases of serious injury at school, so too do they have the right to secure crisis services for suicidal youth when parents cannot be contacted. Schools are not financially responsible for the costs of hospitalization or emergency evaluation services under these conditions (Ruof & Harris, 1988c).

Face-to-Face Interview

Inform parents of the behaviors and warning signs that led to their child's referral to a crisis team member. The team member should share some of the student's responses to interview questions in order to highlight the need for intervention.

It is critical that school personnel refrain from implying that the parents are to blame for their child's condition. Conveying judgments (even if they are justified) will create anger and defensiveness rather than cooperation. Instead, every effort should be made to emphasize the positive role parents can play to help their child. They need to understand that what they say and do can have a major impact on how their child will cope.

Always anticipate possible parental defensiveness when a student's behavior is maladaptive. The initial parental interview, conducted without the child being present, generally will permit open and honest communication with parents. If the child is not present, parents may be more honest about the child's problems, especially if they are given objective indicators about their child's difficulties (e.g., declining academic performance; acting out; substance abuse). Being empathic and supportive in communications with parents will help elicit their cooperation. Parental cooperation is also enhanced by framing a student's inappropriate behavior as a cry for parental help, rather than as an implied criticism of the parents.

In cases where there is a divorce (or pending divorce) and both parents are present, there is a possibility that the parents will engage in blaming one another for their child's condition. The crisis team member should *never* be drawn into taking sides. Every effort should be made to point out to both parents that continued acrimonious exchanges are not in the best interests of their child, especially during this crisis. If the hostile exchange continues, it may be necessary to separate the parents and hold individual meetings with each. If agreeable, it may be best to ask the parent with whom the child is living to remain, and to schedule a separate appointment with the other parent.

School professionals should provide concrete suggestions for parents to help defuse the present crisis. Below are our suggestions for school personnel working with the parents of students in crisis:

- Be directive if outside agencies need to be involved. Specify how, when, and who parents must contact. Also discuss transportation to the agency, including whether parents would like school personnel to accompany them with their child. If parents lack a means of transportation, obtain parental permission for the school to transport the student in a district vehicle.

- Ask parents to sign a release-of-information form to allow for the exchange of confidential information between the school and community agency. Explain that this is in the best interest of the student because it will aid cooperation between the school and the agency.

- Ask parents to immediately remove any lethal means from the home (e.g., guns, pills). Tell parents to let their child know why they are removing potentially lethal suicidal methods (e.g., "Keeping you alive is all that matters to us. We're removing _____ because we don't want you to hurt yourself. We care very much what happens to you.").

- Tell parents to not leave their child unsupervised for any length of time until additional help is secured. After outside intervention has been initiated, parents still need to be alert for signs of unhealthy isolation (e.g., constantly staying in room; avoiding family or peer activities), and for signs of depression (e.g., sleep or appetite disturbance; crying jags). If these signs persist, ask parents to inquire directly about suicidal thinking (e.g., "Have you been thinking of suicide again?").

- Ask parents about stressors in their child's life. Together, brainstorm ways to reduce stress. Emphasize that predictability and consistency are important, and to make sure that the child is eating and sleeping properly.

- Encourage parents to listen to their child and refrain from interrupting, arguing, defending, lecturing, or chastising. However, parents do need to set clear limits on inappropriate behavior. This should be done in a calm and non-combative manner. Stress to the parents the importance of avoiding the escalation of conflicts.

- Encourage parents to emphasize their child's strengths. Because low self-esteem is often associated with a personal crisis, parents need to consider ways to enhance their child's views of self. Similarly, ask parents to verbally express love for their child (e.g., "I love you very much and would never want to lose you.").

- Encourage parents to engage in positive activities with their children. Although parents cannot force a recalcitrant teenager to communicate with them, they can create opportunities for intimate sharing to take place. These moments often occur naturally during the course of such activities as taking a walk together, playing games, or going out to dinner. Although children will not always respond to parental overtures to help or to communicate, just knowing that parents are concerned and available can be critical. However, parents should be cautioned not to give up or to lash out if their initial overtures are rejected. Their child may be willing to reach out or accept support the next time it is offered.

- Parents can and should be powerful role models of adaptive problem solving and stress management. Ask parents to "think aloud" in front of their children when faced with a problem or stressor. Encourage them to talk about why they select a particular approach to problem solving, the emotions they experience, and how they cope with failures.

- Ask parents to find opportunities to reinterpret their child's sense of inadequacy by reframing perceived failures as valued learning experiences. Also encourage parents to provide a "reality check" on the irrational and self-deprecating beliefs of their children (e.g., I should have . . ., I never . . ., I always . . .).

- Inform parents that a seemingly dramatic improvement in the adolescent's mood and behavior (within a span of a few hours) may be cause for alarm. This can be a sign that the youth has decided to commit suicide or take other drastic action (e.g., run away).

- Provide parents with a list of helping resources (e.g., books, videos, special community programs, social service agencies).

After making these suggestions, the parents and student should be seen together. Before bringing the student into the meeting, however, the interviewer should emphasize two things. First, encourage each parent to express to the child their love, concern, and support. Second, if parents agree with the assessment and the recommendations of the crisis response team, they should tell their child that they are in agreement. Parents and school personnel need to present a "united front," particularly when the student appears reluctant to seek help.

Parental Non-cooperation

Some parents will not take any protective actions to secure their child's safety, even after being presented with clear evidence of suicidal risk. When parents deny or refuse to accept clear evidence of risk, their children have an increased probability of attempting suicide. For this reason, Poland and Pitcher (1990) recommend letting parents know that refusing to seek services for their child, in the face of compelling evidence of suicidal potential, can be considered neglect by the child welfare department. In such cases, the school has a legal and professional responsibility to file such a charge if parents fail to act appropriately. Such strong action by the school should be used only as a last resort. Poland and Pitcher have found that mentioning the possibility of contacting Child Protective Services convinces almost all parents to follow the course of protective action delineated by the school or mental health professional. While such measures may temporarily alienate the parents, it may also save the child's life.

Sometimes the danger is so great that the possibility of filing a neglect charge, without taking other protective measures, is not enough. The student may require immediate hospitalization or psychiatric services which are beyond the capacity of the school to deliver. A partial list of examples adapted from Motto (1978) which require immediate action include the following:

- the student has just made a suicide attempt at school;

- the student has a specific suicide plan, refuses to contract, and is isolated from sources of help;

- the student expresses an inability to resist acting upon the suicidal impulse;

- the student is undergoing a psychotic episode;

- the suicidal state is drug induced (e.g., following consumption of psychedelic drugs).

Once again, never leave a student alone who is in such a state. A crisis team member or other adult should wait with the student until additional help is available. Some schools have an arrangement with the local police to drive the student to a community mental health agency or hospital for further evaluation. In an emergency, many law enforcement officials can assume protective custody of a student for a limited period of time (e.g., 48-72 hours).

The Department of Social Services or other designated community agency also can take temporary custody of a student if the danger of suicide seems imminent and parents are uncooperative. In such instances, an evaluation of the need for hospitalization is often ordered by the police or child welfare officials. It is therefore important for the school to develop collaborative emergency procedures with the police or other agencies prior to a crisis.

It is also important for the crisis team to have available a list of community agencies and professionals in private practice who specialize in suicide crisis intervention. Crisis team members should know the following about those listed: (1) referral procedures; (2) fees for services; (3) availability on short notice, including after hours and on weekends; and (4) procedures for releasing information.

Parents sometimes will refuse to allow school or community professionals to talk to their children after the initial risk assessment interview. In some states, minors can receive professional counseling without parental consent, particularly in cases of an emergency. In

Michigan, for example, students fourteen-years-old and older may receive up to twelve sessions of therapy at a community mental health agency without parental permission. Reimbursement for services is on an ability to pay basis. Texas also passed legislation which authorizes school personnel, without parental consent, to provide psychological services to minors at risk of suicide (Poland, 1989). School officials should check the guidelines of their state or province to determine appropriate action.

Our position here is clear: do whatever is deemed professionally necessary to secure services for students in imminent danger of suicide.   Given the potential for litigation in this area, however, it is prudent for school personnel to be familiar with relevant state legislation, the guidelines of professional organizations representing school personnel, and the legal opinion of the school district's attorney regarding the provision of services in the absence of parental permission.

Follow-up

Whether a suicidal student is hospitalized or engaged in outpatient therapy, there is a need for the school, the parents, and community professionals to communicate with one another. Informational exchanges should clarify their respective roles regarding the needs of the student.

Our view is that school personnel are not in the position to provide long-term treatment to suicidal students. Even so, it is important for a member of the school's crisis response team to take responsibility for acting as a liaison to agencies working with the student, and to monitor how the student is doing in school and at home. Follow-up by school personnel should serve two purposes: ensure that high risk students continue receiving the help they need, and alert the school and the parents if there is an escalation in suicidal thinking or behavior.

Johnson and Maile (1987) advise educators to consider the difficult issues with which students must grapple when they return to school following a suicide attempt.   These include returning to a stress-producing environment, facing peers, teachers and others who know about what has happened, and trying to avoid relapse while coping with the problems that initially led to the suicide attempt.   Johnson and Maile emphasize the importance of the school as a positive "holding environment" where normalcy, consistency, predictability, and acceptance can aid in recovery.

Providing such a holding environment may entail assigning one member of the crisis response team to act as an in-school case manager for the student.   The case manager would take responsibility for organizing the school's follow-up activities for a minimum of six months after the initial suicidal crisis (Ryerson & King, 1986).

One follow-up activity should be to plan meetings with the student's teachers, counselors or other appropriate staff.   The purpose is to review ways to reduce school stress and meet the student's needs for safety, structure, and acceptance (Ryerson & King, 1986).   At these meetings, encourage teachers to be alert for changes in the student's academic performance, attitudes, or interactions with peers, and report these to the case manager.   It is the responsibility of the case manager to then report to the parents.

School staff also should be encouraged to initiate contacts with the student (e.g., before or after class or school) that are warm and friendly, but not overly solicitous or probing. The goal of these contacts is to serve two functions: keeping the channel of communication open between the student and caring adults, and reducing academic or other problems which are producing stress.

It is also recommended that the case manager periodically meet with the student to reassess the student's overall state of health or well-being. Specifically, the case manager may wish to ask the following questions.

- Is the stress in your life now the same as when you were feeling suicidal? More ? Less?

- Are you still going to therapy? Is it helpful?

- Who would you identify as part of your current support system? Has your support system changed since you were feeling suicidal? In what ways?

- Do you still think of suicide as an option? If yes, how often? When? How long ago?

The case manager's purpose in asking these questions is *not* to take on the role of therapist. Rather, risk assessment should be more than a one-time event with suicidal youth. *Brief periodic interviews over time are an effective way to monitor behavior and to ensure that the level of risk is not increasing.*

If the case manager suspects the student's risk level is increasing, then the community professionals and the parents should be contacted. Even when the risk is not increasing, however, engaging in periodic contact with the student's parents usually is beneficial. Such contact allows the school professional to offer assistance to parents who have child-rearing concerns or communication problems with their offspring. It also allows the case manager to more thoroughly monitor the level of risk by obtaining information from parents about their child's mood, behavior, and coping skills.

In contacts with parents, if it is clear that parental behavior is functioning to increase the risk to their child, the school has no choice but to notify proper authorities. For example, if there is strong suspicion of physical or sexual abuse, or if there is constant parental substance abuse, these are the very conditions which may be at the root of the student's crisis. The school's guidelines for reporting child abuse or neglect should shape the actions of school personnel in such cases.

In most cases, however, parents will want to cooperate with school professionals if they see that it is in the best interests of their child. Regularly sharing information with the parents, in an honest and forthright manner, is the first step in securing that cooperation.

8
IMPLEMENTING A
POSTVENTION PROTOCOL

What impact do suicides have on the behaviors of students and staff in a school? How should schools respond to a suicide? What kinds of contingency plans should schools establish to prepare for the suicide of a student or teacher?

To date, there has been relatively little study of how schools cope with suicide. We are aware of no national studies in the United States or Canada which systematically evaluate school crisis response plans, or for that matter, accurately determine how many school districts have such plans in place. Yet suicide is a violent and shocking event which has a dramatic impact on school climate and on behavior. When a member of the school community commits suicide, the competencies of many students can be impaired, normal educational routines can be suspended, and the safety and mental well-being of many students may be threatened.

Despite the importance of preparing for a tragedy, however, the creation and implementation of plans in preparation for a suicide induced crisis is a new phenomenon for many schools. Because suicide is a relatively rare event, few schools have adequate plans to address the myriad problems that arise following such a dramatic event. Schools need emergency plans which clarify the activities necessary for all personnel to follow in the wake of a suicide.

But progress is being made. In the past few years educators and others have developed a keen interest in school postvention efforts following a self-inflicted death. Recently, for example, the American Association of Suicidology published its recommended postvention guidelines for schools. Furthermore, a handful of states have mandated that schools prepare for the possibility of youth suicide by requiring teachers, counselors and other school personnel to receive training in the recognition of warning signs and in crisis intervention. Now many school districts are wisely organizing crisis teams designed to coordinate recovery efforts in the event of a tragedy.

These are hopeful signs. Presently, however, many school districts have yet to adopt comprehensive and flexible policies to guide them in the aftermath of a suicide or other tragedy (e.g., murder). Few school boards have adopted step-by-step guidelines for educators to follow, even though the school often becomes the focal point of community concern in the wake of a student's act of self-destruction.

Even when crisis plans exist, they often are on paper only and have never been communicated to those expected to implement them. Furthermore, planning for a crisis (which admittedly may never happen) requires allocation of scarce resources, a commitment to maintain crisis response teams, and a continuing system of inservice training. However, crisis inservice training for staff is limited or nonexistent in many schools. Moreover, collaboration between schools and community agencies — an essential prerequisite to successful crisis intervention — is easier said than done, especially if there is no history of such collaboration in other areas.

Some might argue that expenditure of time and resources in preparation for a remote contingency is a "frill," especially when budgets are being cut and citizens are demanding that schools get "back to basics." Yet the alternative to developing and implementing crisis response plans means committing the school to inaction and confusion at a time when clear thinking and swift decisions are required. Lack of crisis planning can undermine the educational mission of schools; it can also place some students at risk of additional harm. Not only is such risk avoidable, but it also raises the specter of school liability because of negligence. Therefore it is critical that each school have in place a plan to deal with the aftermath of traumatic loss. As many experts have noted, *a postvention policy is one of the best methods of preventing further risk of harm.*

Postvention Planning

The school's response to a suicide should seek to accomplish several broad goals. Included here are the following:

- Efforts should be directed toward individual and collective grief resolution.

- Attention should be given to reducing the risk of additional traumatic loss or injury (e.g., another suicide; retaliation for the death).

- High priority should be given by school staff to rebuilding a sense of community following the death.

- Postvention activities should focus on allowing the school to resume normal activities as soon as possible after the suicide, while maintaining an appropriate follow-up program which reduces potential risks to students and staff.

If schools accomplish these goals, then the competencies of students and staff will not be undermined. Indeed, appropriate action following a tragedy can *strengthen* the competencies of many. But inaction, or well-intentioned efforts which are poorly planned, will only add to the school community's trauma.

CRISIS RESPONSE PROTOCOL

In developing a plan to accomplish these objectives, schools should follow several guiding principles. First, educators should do nothing which romanticizes or glamorizes suicide. Second, procedures to guide decision-making should be in place *before* a tragedy occurs, rather than emerging during a crisis. Finally, in order to respond effectively to the needs of students, help must first be given to the faculty who are in direct contact with students and parents (Lamb & Dunne-Maxim, 1987). With these principles in mind, the following are practical guidelines for schools to follow when tragedy strikes. In preparing these guidelines, we credit and build upon the work of the following authors who have made excellent suggestions regarding postvention: American Association of Suicidology, 1991; Davis and Sandoval, 1991; Fairfax

County Public Schools, 1987; Lamb & Dunne-Maxim, 1987; Patros & Shamoo, 1989; Rouf et al. 1987.

Before a Crisis

At the building level, each school should decide in advance who will be in charge if a suicide takes place. Usually this is the principal, though a substitute should be designated if the principal is unavailable. Staff roles should be delineated such that each staff member is clear as to his or her responsibilities (e.g., principal communicates with parents, teachers monitor student behavior for problems, library staff provides information resources for staff, students and parents).

Each school should make space available for meetings following a crisis. Included here are rooms for individual and small group sessions. A counseling center (or centers) should be established in anticipation of a tragedy.

Administrators, teachers and support staff should have inservice training in how to respond in the aftermath of a suicide. This inservice training should be a continuing effort; it should be included as part of a comprehensive approach to dealing with students at risk.

At the district level, crisis response teams should be formed. Both educators and community professionals could be included on the teams. The superintendent or other designated district official should work closely with the teams in order to issue directives in a crisis. The primary responsibilities of such teams include coordination of recovery efforts, evaluation of crisis intervention efforts, and keeping the lines of communication open throughout the school.

Addressing the Immediate Crisis

When first hearing of a suicide or other traumatic crisis, the principal should verify this information with the police or other appropriate officials. Accurate information is essential in order to combat the "rumor mill."

Upon verification, persons within the school system and community — on a need to know basis — should be notified immediately. These include crisis team members, the superintendent, teachers, and support staff such as counselors, school psychologists, and school nurses. A prearranged telephone chain should be activated upon confirmation of the event.

If a suicide occurs after school hours or on a weekend, notification of building personnel should be done as soon as possible. When staff are called, they should be told of an emergency meeting before the arrival of students the next school day (e.g., 45 minutes before school starts). If news of a tragedy is received during school hours, the faculty meeting should be scheduled immediately after school. Students who are family members of the deceased should be brought to the principal's office or counseling center to meet with parents or other responsible adults. If there are siblings in other schools, the principals of those schools should be notified.

The principal should assemble the crisis response team and invite to this meeting any community professionals capable of helping the school deal with the tragedy (e.g., mental health clinicians, clergy). It is the team's responsibility to determine the scope of postvention efforts. Some tragedies have considerably more impact than others (e.g., death of a popular student *vs.* death of a new transfer student whom few others know). The intensity of postvention efforts should match the degree of impact the event is likely to have on the school community. At the meeting, the team should review all necessary steps to coordinate the school's response, and assign tasks accordingly (see *Appendix A* for a complete crisis response team checklist).

The emergency staff meeting presents an opportunity to review known facts surrounding the incident, and to dispel rumors. Procedures for teachers and staff to follow during the first hour (see *Appendix B*) and throughout the day should be discussed. Included here are guidelines for announcing the death to students. The crisis response team should describe the common thoughts, feelings, and behaviors many people experience following a tragedy, and then suggest ways for school staff to respond. It is important that the team identify which student reactions warrant immediate referral, including warning signs of impending suicide intent. The procedure for referring students to support services should be made clear. Before the end of the staff meeting, a decision should be made as to whether the school is to maintain its normal schedule, or whether modifications need to be made.

Certain teachers or other staff may need special help. As suggested by Rouf et al. (1987), these may be persons who were particularly close to the suicide victim, or who recently disciplined the deceased, or who may have failed to act on prior knowledge which could have helped to avert a crisis. These staff members should not be expected to deal with the emotional problems of students if they are unable to handle their own emotions. Provision should be made to offer them separate counseling and coverage for their classes as needed.

Close friends of the deceased, including a boyfriend or girlfriend, should be taken aside when they arrive at school and informed privately before other students are notified. This group of intimate friends should be invited to meet at a selected site to discuss what has happened and to receive help from a crisis team member. Given that these students are likely to have special needs, it is critical that they be given more intense attention.

No student should be allowed to leave school, unless they are released to a parent or guardian who is aware of what has happened. Students who leave should be monitored upon their return to school and referred to support services if needed.

At the beginning of the first class, teachers should announce what has happened. To help them, the principal should provide teachers with a prepared statement. The statement should be a straightforward explanation with an emphasis on the expression of condolences. The information presented should be truthful, but without elaboration of graphic details. Being truthful limits potentially harmful speculation while encouraging a climate of open communication. Open discussion should allow for the expression of grief, while discouraging speculation or the tendency to assign blame.

Where possible, the best procedure is to discuss the death in the confines of the classroom, rather than over the public address system or in a large assembly. The classroom constitutes a more intimate setting where it is possible to monitor the reactions of students more easily. Large groups are very impersonal and too unmanageable for helping students to process their feelings. Prompt acknowledgment of the situation in a controlled environment where it is acceptable to express feelings is the ideal.

Inform students that adults who can help are available in designated counseling areas. Anticipate a range of student reactions: shock, anger, disbelief, and crying are common examples. Some students may need to be escorted to a designated area for help; most others will prefer to remain in class. Any student known to have had prior knowledge of the deceased's suicidal intentions should receive individual attention by a crisis team member.

Communicate to students that information regarding a memorial service will be given as soon as it is available. Students should be discouraged from seeking information by contacting the family of the deceased.

Following the announcement, teachers should allow for open dialogue and the expression of grief in their classes. Those teachers who feel uncomfortable with discussing the death should request the help of a crisis team member or other appropriate support person. Crisis team members should be prepared to cover classes for teachers too distraught to deal with what has happened, or to otherwise help teachers in leading classroom discussions. Any attempt by students to romanticize or to define suicide as a heroic act should be strongly discouraged.

As the day progresses, expressions of grief and discussion time may be necessary in each class. Major tests or reviews should be postponed for at least several days. In those classes where the deceased would have been present, a crisis team member or other adult should occupy the seat and share in discussions. It is important for students to feel that help is available to them — both individually and in groups — throughout the day. It is also important for students to feel a climate where honest and open dialogue is possible. Traumatic events bring up a great deal of unfinished business in peoples' lives; open communication helps to resolve such conflicts.

A school representative from the building or the district, accompanied by a crisis team member, should make contact with the family of the deceased to express condolences and to offer support. Arrangements should be made to return the contents of the student's locker or other possessions. The family's wishes regarding students and school staff visiting the funeral home or attending the funeral should be respected. Some families will prefer a closed service; others will be amenable to student attendance. Announcement of funeral arrangements should be made at school. If students receive permission to visit the funeral home or to attend the service, a crisis team member should be present.

At the end of the first day, a staff meeting should be held to review events (see *Appendix C* for meeting guidelines). Crisis team members should be present to offer feedback and to provide support. This debriefing is important for several reasons. First, it allows staff members to verbalize their feelings and to build solidarity. Second, it reinforces the sharing of ideas for working effectively with students. Third, it allows staff to plan the next day's activities. Finally, this process may help identify students who are suffering from problems which have surfaced due to the crisis. Such meetings should continue periodically for several weeks after the death.

After a suicide, any commemorative or other observances at school for the deceased should be given a low profile. Well-intentioned responses such as flying the flag at half mast, displaying a memorial plaque, dedicating the yearbook, or planting a 'suicide memorial' tree should not be considered. (Such gestures are more appropriate following an accidental death.) Dramatic gestures of loss add to the danger of making suicide attractive, serving to mystify the event, thereby allowing it to take on heroic dimensions. Commemorative activities should be channeled in a more positive direction (e.g., doing volunteer work, donating blood to the Red Cross, raising money for a worthy cause).

If the funeral is scheduled during school hours, the school should remain open. Arrangements should be made to cover the classes of faculty wishing to attend. At least one administrator and crisis team member should be present to represent the school and to provide support. Students attending should have written permission from their parents. If the funeral is held during the weekend, parents should be encouraged to attend the service with their children in order to monitor their reactions.

If the suicide occurred on school grounds, school officials should immediately seal off the area in question. The location should be professionally cleaned so as to leave no trace of the incident. In the days following the death, crisis team members may wish to take note of any students who seem to linger in the area. Often these students are those most affected by the event and who are most in need of help.

Working with the Media

The news media will always take an interest in the "story" of a crisis, yet sensationalizing a tragedy poses problems for schools. How much media access to school grounds and to school personnel, if any, should administrators permit in the aftermath of a suicide? What are the consequences of alienating the media in an attempt to protect vulnerable persons who might suffer as a result of media coverage? How can school officials minimize the negative consequences of intense (and often critical) media coverage?

Given that the news media can increase the risk of contagion or "copy cat" behavior due to carelessness in reporting a story, school officials are well-advised to be cautious in presenting information to reporters. This does not mean that schools should avoid contact with reporters. Rather, school officials should be concerned that sensitive information and sensationalization can increase the risk for vulnerable students and families. School officials also must be sensitive to reporters' needs to present information to the public. Failure to work effectively with the media may unintentionally communicate the message that the school is in a state of chaos, and that the safety of children is in jeopardy. The balanced approach is to answer media questions accurately without disclosing unnecessary or confidential information.

We strongly recommend that a press release plan be established before a tragedy occurs. Statements to the media should be brief and factual, highlighting the school's proactive response to the crisis. Speculative opinion should be avoided. We also concur with the recommendation of the American Association of Suicidology (1991) that a single spokesperson (e.g., the principal) be designated by the school or district to answer questions. Other staff should refer questions from the media to the official spokesperson. In addition, the American Association of Suicidology recommends that schools discourage the media from the following: specifying details of the suicide method; using the word "suicide" on the front-page or other headlines; or printing photographs of the deceased. They also advise the following:

> "The school should avoid becoming the principal source of information. Releasing details about the suicide is the responsibility of the medical examiner or other authorities. Never permit speculation as to why the student committed suicide. It is the family's sole prerogative to provide information about the victim" (American Association of Suicidology, 1991).

There are a number of other considerations for schools in their relationship to the media. We recommend the following.

- Because bright lights, cameras, and reporters can be very disconcerting while attempting to calmly present accurate information, the designated spokesperson should periodically practice doing video tape sessions. Practice before a camera helps to prepare one for these tense conditions.

- In advance of any type of crisis, and as a normal part of school-community collaboration, the school should regularly submit information to the media about new programs, special events, and other successful activities.

- Schools can avert problems by setting guidelines in advance for working with the media in the event of a crisis. The school's right to protect students and faculty from possible risk and from unwanted intrusion should be stressed. Schools are within their rights to place restrictions on media access to staff and students during school hours and on school property. Likewise, the media's right to know and to report responsibly should also be stressed. If appropriate, school and media representatives should agree in advance that interviews with persons other than the designated spokesperson will be conducted away from school premises. This reduces inappropriate access to students and staff, and minimizes the possibility of creating a circus atmosphere in the midst of a crisis.

- Develop and periodically update a list of names and addresses of local media representatives. In the event of a crisis, a factual press release should be distributed to them. The name of the official spokesperson should be included, and ground rules for interviews should be specified.

- Set the parameters of press conferences in advance, including where and for how long school officials will meet media representatives. It is appropriate for school officials to raise concerns about the impact news stories can have on other students and on the family of the deceased. Sensationalizing suicides (or murders) can adversely affect school efforts to help in the recovery process.

- School officials should eschew any hint that they are in a state of panic or that there is a cover up. Certainly the school's reputation — and the students who are affected by the crisis — will suffer if educators suggest that their primary interest is in protecting the school's image. This means that arguing with reporters, finding scapegoats, delays in sharing information, and making "off the record" or "no comment" remarks are to be avoided.

- One advantage of media coverage is that the community has an opportunity to receive important messages about suicide warning signs, about sources of help, and about the school's suicide prevention efforts (American Association of Suicidology, 1991; Poland, 1989). It is therefore worthwhile for schools to prepare written materials which highlight the positive steps being taken by the school and by community agencies. Providing practical information about what people can do and where they can secure help promotes responsible journalism, reduces panic, and contributes to rebuilding a sense of community.

Follow-up After the Crisis

School protocol and classroom interactions should resume a sense of normalcy within a few days of the tragedy. While it is important for school staff to be caring and supportive, it is also important that they convey a sense of predictability, consistency, and control.

Following the death, the crisis team should continue to meet daily for as long as necessary in order to process student referrals, and to assess the continuing impact of the tragedy on the school community. Depending upon the intensity of the event, the crisis team must decide how long to continue support services at the school, and when referral to community professionals is appropriate.

In the weeks and months following a suicide, there should be several joint meetings with staff and crisis team members for the purpose of evaluation. Information should be exchanged as to how all levels of the school are coping. Staff should be alert to the possibility of delayed grief reactions experienced by students. The effects of a traumatic death are likely to linger; some people who initially show little emotion can be greatly affected at a later time. Special consideration should be given to these students and to the best friends of the deceased.

One of the most important things a school can do following a suicide is to encourage student involvement in a survivors group. Such groups are especially valuable to students who are family members or intimate friends of the deceased. Given limited school resources, however, collaboration between the school and an appropriate community agency in developing survivors groups usually is necessary.

Sharing information with concerned parents should be done in a low key manner rather than in a large open meeting (Lamb & Dunne-Maxim, 1987). Large assemblies tend to heighten already charged emotions. Making persons available to speak with these parents individually or in small groups is appropriate. (In tragedies not involving suicide, the school may wish to sponsor an open meeting with interested parents.) The goal of such communication is to afford parents the opportunity to share feelings, to gain an understanding of the school's response, and to discuss coping strategies which could benefit them and their children. Oftentimes such communications following a crisis set the stage for improved relations between the school and the home.

As educators plan their follow-up efforts, it is important to anticipate a range of student reactions (Lamb & Dunne-Maxim, 1987). For the first week or so, educators should expect an emotionally charged atmosphere (see *Appendix D* for guidelines on minimizing the stress associated with such a critical incident). Initial responses to news of a student or teacher suicide include shock, denial, disbelief, grief, confusion, and possibly anger. The anger in particular will be pronounced if it is believed that "someone was to blame" for what happened, if school officials seem insensitive, or if they tend to "stonewall" about the reality of the event. Anger and the tendency to scapegoat, however, can be minimized if school officials quickly disseminate accurate information and have in place a plan to manage the situation.

As the school gradually returns to its pre-crisis routines, many will continue to struggle with what has happened. Faculty who work with those student and parents most distressed by the suicide are likely to become emotionally exhausted. For the next several months, therefore, it is important to hold regular staff meetings which are especially sensitive to staff needs. This also may be a time to encourage some staff to take one or more "personal days" in order to reduce the tendency for them to be overwhelmed. Encouraging open dialogue and providing support to faculty during this period will build an *"esprit de corps."*

It is especially important to have periodic debriefing sessions for crisis team members. These debriefings might best be conducted jointly by mental health professionals and school or district staff who are *not* part of the crisis team (see *Appendix D*). Caution must be taken so that the crisis team does not become overwhelmed.

Throughout the year, school personnel should continue to be vigilant. Often seemingly lesser problems will reactivate unresolved issues associated with the suicide. Both anniversary dates and happy occasions (e.g., the prom or graduation) are particularly volatile for some and can trigger renewed feelings of loss. Possibly those students still struggling with unresolved issues can be identified and helped at these times. During these special times, continued outreach directed toward the close friends and family members of the deceased may be appropriate and should be built in to the school's long-term follow-up plans.

It is obvious that prior planning and careful follow-up can minimize the dangers inherent in a crisis caused by a suicide. Unfortunately, all too often schools are in the position of having their postvention efforts evolve in the midst of a crisis, rather than being in place before a tragedy. Even when postvention plans exist, they may be used so infrequently that they are outdated or difficult to implement because key persons have never rehearsed their roles in advance. It therefore pays for each school to develop and rehearse plans and procedures in anticipation of a crisis. A comprehensive postvention plan is essential if schools are to minister to student needs and to reduce the risk of suicide contagion.

9
REDUCING SUICIDE
CONTAGION

When a student commits suicide, it can have a potent modeling effect on peers by providing tacit permission for emulation. The spread of suicidal ideas and behaviors from student to student is called contagion; it is directly associated with what experts refer to as a "cluster suicide." The Centers for Disease Control (1988) defines a suicide cluster as "a group of suicides or suicide attempts, or both, that occur closer together in time and space than would normally be expected in a given community."

Many scholars believe that as a group, adolescents are vulnerable to suicide contagion. This is especially true for those students who are already prone to suicide due to deep feelings of hopelessness. Similar to other students who may develop suicidal impulses, research by Ruof et al. (1987), as well as our own assessment (McEvoy & McEvoy, 1990), suggests that the risk of contagion increases if a student:

- is a relative or close friend of the person who committed suicide;

- has agreed to a suicide pact with the victim;

- was with the deceased shortly before or during the suicide;

- believes he or she said or did things which directly contributed to a peer's suicide;

- knew about or suspected the suicidal plan but did not act on this knowledge;

- is seriously abusing drugs or alcohol;

- has a previous history of suicide attempts;

- had a significant recent loss and is experiencing unresolved conflicts provoked by the suicide;

- has experienced recent family disruption (e.g., divorce);

- comes from a seriously abusive or dysfunctional home;

- has a weak or nonexistent social support system (e.g., a social isolate) and feels hopelessly overwhelmed by problems;

- has a history of depression and impulsivity, or exhibits mental instability;

- identifies strongly with the suicide victim for reasons such as shared interests or social activities, or similar family histories.

Although the phenomenon is not well understood, it appears that "modeling effects" are an important element in suicide contagion among adolescents. Students who are already experiencing some crisis when a peer (or family member) commits suicide may then emulate this suicidal behavior, perhaps because it now appears to them as a clear "solution" to personal difficulties. This modeling effect can be especially powerful if the peer was popular or admired, if the peer ended his or her life in a spectacular way, or if the deceased was someone with whom the students strongly identified (Ruof et al. 1987).

In considering the risks of contagion, schools are confronted with a major dilemma. On the one hand, educators cannot immediately return to normal routines following a student suicide. To do so would ignore the needs of those who may be at highest risk. On the other hand, educators do not want to overreact by dramatizing the event. To do so may further increase the risk of suicide. With this dilemma in mind, what can schools do to minimize contagion?

DIMINISHING THE RISKS

Suicide contagion cannot occur if students are unaware of a peer's suicide. It sometimes happens that only a few students know or are concerned about the suicide (perhaps in the case of a former pupil or a new transfer student). If appropriate, provide individual help only to those peers affected. Encourage these students to express their concerns directly to a counselor or other professional rather than to fellow students. A crisis team member or other designated staff member should explain to them about the dangers of spreading rumors. If it is not possible to contain rumors, then it may be necessary to implement the regular suicide crisis response protocol, or at least an abridged version of it.

In most cases, however, a student's death will soon be known throughout the school and will be a source of deep concern. The task for educators is to control the flow of information so as to avoid a state of panic. In order to accomplish this, teachers should read a memo to all students during the first hour of classes. This memo should be written by the principal or by a crisis team member.

Contained in the memo should be a summary of relevant public information. If the exact cause of death has not yet been determined, include only what is known for certain. The memo should provide:

- documented facts about the event (without speculation or graphic detail);

- a statement of regret over the loss;

- details on available supportive services;

- information about school policy and any changes in school schedules;

- information regarding memorial services (or a promise to provide such information once arrangements are confirmed).

Sample Memo to Students

We have just learned that John Doe, a student in the 11th grade, died yesterday. We are all deeply saddened by his death; the suddenness of it is a shock to us all.

Support services for students are available and will be discussed in detail later this hour. The hall pass policy has been altered for today. Students wishing to talk to a crisis response team member will be given a pass; they are to proceed directly to room _____ .

The funeral arrangements have not yet been completed. Information regarding memorial services will be made known when the arrangements are confirmed. All of us offer our sincerest condolences to John's family and friends.

The school also should communicate promptly with all students' parents following a student suicide. Parents will be concerned for their children and will need information about ways to help.

The simplest method for communicating with them is to send a letter home with each student the same day the death is announced at school. If the death occurred during summer or Christmas break, then letters should be mailed to each family once details are confirmed.

Similar to notifying students, the letter to parents should:

- verify the death;

- express regret;

- indicate available support services to help their children;

- specify any changes in school scheduling;

- provide information about the memorial service.

One value of prompt communication with parents is that their help can be enlisted in school efforts to prevent contagion.

Sample Letter to Parents

Dear Parent or Guardian:

_____ High School experienced a tragic loss in the death of John Doe, an 11th grade student at our school. All of us are deeply saddened. The suddenness of his death is a shock to us all.

Our crisis response team is working with community professionals to provide counseling services to students and others affected by John's death. We also are encouraging students to talk to their parents about any concerns related to this tragic loss.

Because no one can predict exactly how students will react, your help is needed. Some students may exhibit behavioral changes and strong emotions such as shock, denial, depression, anger or guilt. Some will be anxious about the safety of their friends. Other students will show no visible change in mood or behavior. Most students will feel a need to talk about the event.

We want to work with you to make sure that your child is safe. If it appears that your son or daughter needs extra help, please call the counseling office at

_____ .

Funeral arrangements are being made. Depending upon the wishes of the family, students will need written permission from parents if there is to be an open service and if it occurs during school hours. If an open service is scheduled during the evening or on the weekend and your child wishes to attend, we strongly recommend that you attend with him or her. Your presence will give you an opportunity to share feelings and to gauge your child's needs.

We express our sincerest condolences to John's family and friends. If the school can assist you in any way, please feel free to call.

Sincerely,

Principal

Given the importance of the school's response in the aftermath of a suicide, many researchers (Centers for Disease Control, 1988; Coleman, 1987; Comstock, Simmons, & Franklin, 1989; Poland, 1989; Ruof et al. 1987; Wenkstern & Leenaars, 1991) have made suggestions for lessening the risk of suicide contagion. Included in the following is our summary of their findings and recommendations, as well as practical suggestions of our own.

Make sure that school or community professionals have identified all students who fall into high risk categories following a peer's suicide. Evaluating their suicide potential is the first step in reducing contagion.

Notify teachers and other appropriate school personnel about students in their care considered to be potentially at risk. Such notification will allow more careful monitoring. It is legally and ethically acceptable to extend the bond of confidentiality to professionals who have a "need to know" under circumstances of a health and safety emergency. The risk of contagion following a suicide constitutes such an emergency.

Discussion of a peer's suicide should proceed in an open and honest manner. Educators should take the initiative in providing opportunities for this discussion to occur within the confines of the classroom rather than in a large assembly. When students are not able to discuss their feelings, then the susceptibility to contagion is greater. In all discussions, however, care should be taken not to romanticize or condone suicidal behavior.

Contact the parents or guardians of all students considered to be at high risk for suicide. Encourage them to communicate with their child about his or her feelings regarding the death. Alert parents to warning signs and inform them of school and community resources for obtaining help. Parents of at-risk students should be contacted periodically for several months following the suicide to ensure that any acceleration of suicidal risk is detected. By maintaining this follow-up, there is an additional benefit to reducing contagion: identification of family or other problems is possible, thus setting the stage for timely interventions.

If possible, limit access to methods or sites used by the deceased. Communicate to parents the importance of making access to firearms, lethal quantities of medication or other hazards unavailable. Enlist the help of law enforcement and other community officials to erect temporary physical barriers to a building, bridge or cliff site used by the victim. It is also important to make sure that any physical evidence of the death (e.g., blood) is removed from the suicide site. Periodic surveillance of the site should also be conducted to reduce the likelihood that students will linger there.

Not only should the school encourage the media to focus their stories on prevention of further suicides rather than on details of the method or motives of the deceased, but the school's internal communications should do the same. Statements to the entire school community, communications to parents and students, and articles in the student newspaper should do the following:

- Specify school prevention initiatives under way or about to be taken.

- Emphasize the situational nature of suicidal thinking. Most young people inclined to suicide are that way for only brief periods of time. Communicate to all students where they can find help. Remind them that there are always alternatives to suicide for coping with pain and for solving emotional crises. Encourage those in need to take the first step by reaching out to others for help. Information about crisis center hotlines and other school and community services should be provided.

- Communicate warning signs that might alert others to those at risk of suicide. Give examples of what to do if one suspects a student is suicidal.

- Remind students that it is *never* appropriate to keep a peer's suicidal intentions a secret. They should immediately seek help if it is believed that a friend is suicidal.

Avoid memorial activities which enshrine the victim. These include closing the school, holding large memorial assemblies, erecting a plaque or planting a memorial tree. Activities which provide meaning and closure are most appropriate (e.g., a contribution to a crisis hotline or suicide prevention center).

Identify and intervene with antagonists of the victim, as well as others feeling responsibility for the death. Guilt is a major factor in imitation suicide. Finally, create psychological distance between the victim and the survivors by highlighting their differences.

There is a note of caution regarding these suggestions to reduce suicide contagion. Well intentioned interventions should not function to produce an atmosphere of melodramatic tragedy and perceived "specialness" which can result in increased emotional intensity and histrionic behavior among students.

To illustrate this point, Callahan (1989) describes a case in one junior high school where, despite implementation of a crisis response protocol following two suicides, a "reverse stigma" was present. Close friends of victims temporarily gained significant status and attention from the suicides because of the interventions directed at them. As a result, student support groups that had been established to assist with postvention were suspended by the second week. Instead, these students were seen individually.

Teachers were understandably concerned about additional suicides. Unfortunately, counselors and other helping staff were slow to provide information to teachers regarding the level of risk for certain students. As a result, too many students were released from classes for long periods of time if they appeared even minimally upset. Students quickly began taking advantage of this procedure.

To counteract this trend, the school responded by having shorter and more focused interventions. Whenever possible, these interventions were scheduled during lunch and study hall. Students were required to make appointments instead of using the counseling office as a "drop in center." Based on assessments conducted by school professionals, teachers were told which students were at highest risk. In addition, high risk students were referred to therapists in the community. A conscious effort also was made to return the primary responsibility for the students' long-term safety back to the parents.

Callahan reported that these limit-setting interventions resulted in a decrease in the amount of contagious suicidal behavior among students. Equally important, the faculty and administration felt more in control.

The school's experience cited by Callahan highlights the need to monitor the effects of school interventions to prevent contagion among students following a peer's suicide. This implies that school postvention efforts should be sufficiently flexible so that timely changes can be made if needed. To do this requires an understanding of student reactions to suicide.

UNDERSTANDING STUDENT REACTIONS

When a student (or teacher) suicide occurs, the risk of contagion can be lessened if educators understand and anticipate student reactions. Many experts point to common student reactions and have suggested appropriate staff responses to students following a suicide (Capuzzi, 1989; Lamb & Dunne-Maxim, 1987; McEvoy & McEvoy, 1990; New Jersey State Department of Human Services, 1989; Poland, 1989; Rouf et al. 1987; Steele, 1992). The following is a summary of how students react and how best to help them.

SHOCK. Some students will be temporarily immobilized when they hear the news of a peer's suicide. They may display little reaction following the announcement because they are in a profound state of psychological shock. School personnel should provide students with an opportunity to talk about the suicide, without forcing them to be open. Some students are ready to talk about their feelings immediately, while for others, it may take much longer to communicate.

DENIAL. Some students may claim that the death was accidental even if it is clearly documented as a suicide. Avoid arguing with them. Present the facts gently, but avoid a debate.

CURIOSITY. Many students will show fascination with details of a suicide. The following questions are common: "How did she do it? Did he die right away? Did she feel any pain? What did he look like when they found him?" Such questions do not mean that students are morbid. If anything, seeking answers is a way to gain greater control. In a known case of suicide, it is important to respond factually (e.g., "She died of carbon monoxide poisoning" or "He died of a gunshot wound to the head"), but do not dwell on the details or possible motives. Respond by stating that such details are less important than helping those who are grieving. Also emphasize that this is an opportunity for all to learn what should and should not be done if they or their friends need help.

If suicide is suspected but not confirmed, do not report it as confirmed without official verification. The following may be an appropriate comment: "We really don't know the reason for the death. Until we know more, it is being considered an accident." In cases where parents request that the school does not share certain information with students, do not reveal anything that is confidential. It may be appropriate to say words to this effect: "I'm sorry, but the parents requested that we not talk about certain details of what has happened. Please understand that rumors will only hurt the family and friends." This may not be possible, however, if information or misinformation is already widely circulated among students.

SEARCH FOR MEANING. The most frequently asked question following a suicide is "WHY?". Do not speculate about the deceased's motivations or the precipitating conditions involved. Simply admit that it is impossible to know all the reasons for a suicide. Emphasize that whatever the reasons, there are always alternatives. Remind students that suicide is a choice. Communicate that no matter how severe one's problems, reaching out to others for help offers solutions. To paraphrase what one teacher told her students, "Most people don't really want to die, they just want to escape their pain. If they get help, they may never be suicidal again. Our task today is to find reasons to keep on living even in the face of pain."

GUILT. Not all students experience guilt (or even intense grief) following the suicide of a peer. Yet two types of students may need special attention: antagonists who bullied, teased or rejected the deceased before the suicide; and close friends of the deceased who may have known about a plan or recognized warning signs, but did not seek help. Students falling into either category should see a crisis team member for individual evaluation.

Staff can help all students by sharing their own feelings of grief. However, a simple reality must prevail in these communications: many students have problems and feel depressed, but they do not kill themselves. Final responsibility for the act must be seen to rest with the deceased. A caring response might be as follows: "There isn't any way to know for sure what would have made a difference. But one thing we all can do now is to offer our friends who are in trouble an alternative by seeking help for them."

BLAMING OTHERS. Survivors of suicide often look for someone to blame — the school, a teacher, the parents, a girlfriend or boyfriend. In particular, students may direct their anger and blame toward school staff when either of two conditions is present. The first condition producing blame is if the school is perceived by students as directly contributing to the deceased's actions (e.g., suspension, expulsion, disciplinary decision, failing the person). The second condition is if the school is perceived as "covering up" or denying the reality of what has happened, even though students feel that they know the "truth."

Remember that their need to ventilate is part of the grief recovery process. Allow their expressions of feeling, but encourage these expressions only under proper circumstances such as in directed individual or group sessions. Student demonstrations or angry letters in the student newspaper are not appropriate channels to express anger. The goal is to diffuse rather than to escalate a charged situation. As such, assigning blame should be discouraged. Again point out that the deceased chose this course, even though alternatives were available. Also point out that many are in pain, and that the sense of loss is shared. You might say, "Now more than ever, there is need to support and help each other, not blame each other."

ANGER TOWARD DECEASED. Some students will express their anger directly at the victim. They will point out how hurtful and selfish the deceased was for taking his or her life, thus leaving the survivors to cope with the aftermath. One way to respond with sensitivity is to explain that persons who take their own lives are not always aware of the devastating impact their death will have on others. Some who commit suicide incorrectly believe that others are better off without them. Remind students that expressions of outrage often have the unintended effect of hurting the victim's family and other loved ones.

ANXIETY. Following a suicide, some students fear for their own safety. A student might think, "If someone like _____ could commit suicide, I probably could too." Some also fear for the safety of their friends. To alleviate anxiety, adults in charge should present a stable and calm demeanor. They should differentiate between thought and action. Students need to know that even if persons occasionally think about suicide, very few act on these thoughts. **Thinking about it does not automatically make it happen.** This is particularly important to emphasize with young adolescents (12-15 years old). Again, stress that suicide is a choice, but not an inevitable choice, and that there are always better alternatives. Remind them that they have the power to help each other and themselves by asking an adult for help. Emphasize that it is *never* appropriate to keep a friend's suicidal thoughts or plans a secret. Empower them with the belief that suicide is preventable.

TEMPORARY DEPRESSION. Experiencing a temporary state of depression is a normal part of the grieving process. The length and depth of this depression will vary depending on one's attachment to the deceased. Do not show impatience with grieving students by exhorting them to "get on with it." If their depression seems prolonged and intense, however, refer them to the crisis team or other appropriate specialists. Furthermore, do not be surprised if depressed students exhibit hostility or aggression. This is sometimes called "masked depression" and often is misinterpreted and mishandled by adults. Although firm limits need to be set on destructive or malicious behavior, discipline should take place in a caring atmosphere.

GLORIFYING SUICIDE. Some students perceive the act of suicide to be brave or heroic. All comments to this effect should be met with the response that it takes greater courage to go on facing problems and to seek solutions. Stress that seeking help is a sign of strength, maturity and courage, and that self-destruction is never heroic.

When students are encouraged to seek help, it is the school's responsibility to make sure that proper help is available. For those students who are most adversely affected by the suicide of a peer or family member, survivors groups can be an important option if they are available.

CREATING SURVIVORS GROUPS

When a student commits suicide, his or her close friends and relatives are the persons most dramatically affected. It is they who are in greatest need of special interventions in order to reduce the spread of suicidal thoughts and behaviors. But when most of us are with the friends or relatives of a suicide victim, we are at a loss for words to offer comfort. What does one say or do to give solace in the face of such loss?

One commonly recommended vehicle for schools to offer comfort and to reduce the likelihood of contagion is to establish "survivors groups." A survivors group is a voluntary assemblage of students who come together for the purpose of coping with grief. The intent is for the group to help the bereaved find ways to communicate about their loss and to find support from others.

The professional literature on suicide, however, is very glib in recommending that schools create survivors groups. It is suggested that their value in helping students is so great that it is imperative for schools to facilitate these groups. Yet it is almost as if this recommendation is an afterthought, tagged onto a long list of other recommendations for schools to follow after a suicide. Almost nothing is said about *how* schools should organize and oversee survivors groups. The practical realities of directing human and other scarce resources to these groups is seldom recognized. Neither is there any mention of potential dangers in such groups.

We agree that survivors groups can be one of the most valuable means of helping students to cope, particularly those who are at highest risk of imitating suicide. We agree that schools should be active in facilitating these groups. But to do this properly, schools need guidance. Simply asserting the importance of school initiatives in this area without providing direction does little to help. Moreover encouraging schools to take action in the midst of a crisis, without giving them specific directions, could result in more harm than good. Creating an effective survivors group in the aftermath of a suicide is tricky business. Careful safeguards and proper supervision are essential. But what should schools do and what should they not do?

Coordinate with Community Mental Health Services

It is better for schools to avoid a commitment to create and maintain survivors groups if they do not have the trained staff to do the job. At least then the school could concentrate attention and resources on those things they know how to do best. If there are to be survivors groups, it is best to have a cooperative plan in place whereby community mental health agencies and the schools work together.

The reality is that few schools have the counseling staff to meet this critical need. As part of a broader collaborative effort, however, the pooling of agency and school *district* resources makes possible the immediate creation of a survivors group after a student suicide. Obtaining resources for establishing and maintaining a survivors group may be the responsibility of the crisis response team.

Once placed in a group, if there is any indication that a student is at imminent risk of suicide, then he or she should be referred immediately to those professionally equipped to respond. Participation in a survivors group alone, without additional supports, is not likely to deter such behavior.

Do Not Mix Groups

Some schools already have in place student support groups for various problems. Often a number of problem areas are mixed together in a single support group. A loved one's suicide, however, poses the unique problem of contagion. It may seem to some as a convenient and efficient "solution" to mix suicide survivors with other self-help groups already in existence at school (e.g., children of divorce groups; children of alcoholics groups). This is a serious mistake. *The immediate needs of the siblings and close friends of those who commit suicide require more intense and specialized help than can be provided through other generic groups. The risk of imitative suicidal behavior is not to be treated in the same way as other problems.*

Another concern is equally critical: *separate groups should be established for those students known to have attempted suicide.* The problems of attempters are not the same as those who are grieving a loss. It is very important that suicidal and other dysfunctional behavior is not modeled, rationalized, or otherwise tacitly accepted as normal in a survivors group. Mixing groups runs this risk. Furthermore, those who are in charge of the group should always keep in mind a basic rule: the purpose is to offer *support*, rather than serving as a substitute for professional *therapy*. As Callahan (1988) notes, group members are "normal individuals who have undergone a traumatic experience, not sick people who require treatment for their own psychopathology."

Provide More than Peer Assistance

Peer assistance programs are an important part of any school effort to help students at risk (see *Chapter 13*). Because suicide contagion constitutes a special problem, however, peer directed assistance groups by themselves are insufficient to meet the needs of those who may be at highest risk of imitative behavior. For example, siblings and close friends of students who commit suicide should be placed in a survivors group (rather than an established peer helping group) *directed by a professional* trained in grief resolution. This could be a mental health specialist from the community or a trained member of the school's crisis team.

Peer leaders, even those with training and experience in group facilitation, cannot and should not perform the intensive group counseling tasks necessary to help students closest to the suicide victim. The immediate needs of survivors require professional expertise. Only after a survivors group has made progress under professional leadership should there be any consideration of linkage with the peer assistance program. The peer assistance program should be considered a valuable long-term adjunct to the survivors group, but it is not a substitute.

Once the survivors group is established, Callahan (1988) suggests weekly meetings for 4-10 weeks, depending upon the need. He recommends that the first session begin with assurances of confidentiality, and that group leaders not press students for an open show of feelings. Rather, students should understand that the group permits the expression of feelings, an opportunity to grieve, and the chance to openly explore the meaning of the death without the expectation that everyone will respond alike.

Offer Long-term Follow-up

The initial counseling needs of family and close friends of suicide victims are likely to be intense for the first several weeks after the incident. This is when close collaboration between schools and community agencies is most critical. Over time, however, survivors groups tend to dissolve naturally.

Because agency commitment to maintaining these groups tends to wane over time, it may be helpful to make survivors groups time-limited (e.g., 8-to-12 weeks). The needs of group members can be re-evaluated at the end of this time to determine the type and extent of follow-up needed.

Some students will need individual long-term follow-up. This may especially be needed during anniversary dates and other significant school events (e.g., the prom) which elicit intense emotions. During these times, directed group sessions for those closest to the deceased are valuable.

Because cluster suicides are preventable, schools are in a good position to take the initiative in reducing the spread of self-destructive thoughts and behaviors. If there is a well-articulated postvention plan in place, coupled with the resources of a trained crisis response team, educators have an excellent chance of preventing contagion. One suicide need not produce more. The lesson is that schools and agencies need to be prepared in order to prevent contagion, and to help the community cope with grief.

10
COPING WITH GRIEF

Grief is a natural response to personal loss; it is characterized by feelings of deep sorrow. Although grieving a loss is normal, this basic emotional response often is misunderstood. For example, grief is sometimes characterized as a "syndrome" which approximates a psychological disorder. Some people suggest an oversimplified view of grief as a series of discrete feelings one experiences in stages over time (e.g., shock, denial, guilt, anger). In truth, grief is neither a psychological disorder, nor does it fit neatly into a progressive series of stages with distinct feelings attached to each stage. Such characterizations are misleading.

True, grief can be psychologically debilitating for both children and adults if it leads to a breakdown of coping skills. Grief may also encompass feelings of shock, denial, guilt, anger and other emotions, though not necessarily in a lock-step series of stages. But grieving need not be entirely negative or debilitating.

It is more accurate to view grief as an emotional process which challenges one's ability to cope with loss while continuing to function. In this sense, grieving poses unique opportunities for a person's growth. Healthy grief resolution means placing the loss in perspective without permanently impairing one's competencies to perform in various roles.   Healthy grief resolution can mean finding inner strengths as one struggles with bereavement.   And healthy grief resolution often unites people in a common bond when they might otherwise have remained divided and isolated.

How one copes with grief, however, and whether grieving results in personal growth or in impairment of competencies, are influenced by the responses of those who communicate with the aggrieved. In this regard, we view the grieving process as a *pattern of interaction* between the individual and others, not merely a psychological condition of the individual. This means that healthy grief resolution — or lack thereof — is largely contingent upon how the aggrieved and others relate to one another.

It is unfortunately true that many people are ill-equipped to communicate effectively with one another when a serious loss occurs. In their desire to help, some give poor advice; some follow poor advice.   For many, pain is prolonged unnecessarily, and the opportunity to assimilate the grief experience as a means of personal growth and as a means of enhancing ties to a community of others is lost.

For educators, the challenges of helping students cope with grief are especially complex if the loss involves the suicide of a classmate or teacher. In the aftermath of such a tragedy, the task for educators is to help their students learn to deal with the loss in a manner which encourages their growth, which reduces the risk of suicide contagion, which promotes a sense of community, and which does not interrupt other educational requirements.

As students mourn the death of a teacher or classmate, they are especially susceptible to the advice they receive from adults whom they have come to trust. Unfortunately, much of the well-intentioned advice given by educators regarding how students should cope with grief is not helpful. Well-intentioned but bad advice is worrisome because it can result in increased risk to the aggrieved. It is therefore essential that teachers, school counselors and others give helpful suggestions to their pupils about how to cope with a tragic loss. Helping students cope with grief is an essential element in a school's postvention efforts.

What Educators Should Know

The first thing educators should know is that the task of helping *individual* students cope with grief is not the same as that of helping students *as a group*. Grief constitutes an element of school climate; it permeates the entire school and affects behavior throughout. This means, for example, that how an individual student responds to a peer's suicide is not necessarily the same as how the student body responds.

Unfortunately, the distinction between the needs of grieving individuals, as opposed to the collective needs of the student body following a tragedy, often is ignored. What most teachers and other school staff need to know is how to help their students in the classroom and in other *group* settings (see *Appendix B* and *D* for guidelines).

Collective grief has a critical distinguishing characteristic: a group feeling a sense of loss tends to create certain tacitly agreed upon rules which shape the members' behavior and which help them to define what the event means. It is the group that gives direction to the perceptions and behaviors of its members. For example, if a particular group (e.g., teachers) is defined by students as being responsible for a peer's act of self-destruction, then conflicts between students and teachers may increase. There may be group pressure for students to act in ways contrary to the wishes of adults and which ultimately compound the process of recovery.

More often, however, conflicts between factions tend to subside for a period following the suicide of a peer. Often there is a greater willingness among members of the school community to show solidarity and to cooperate with one another. The group may reinforce this sense of solidarity by giving tacit permission to publicly show emotions (e.g., hug one another, cry, talk about one's feelings) which otherwise would not occur. For students, such public displays of emotions can be healthy and cathartic, provided that they take place under the guidance of adults capable of effective communication with them. *These public displays should allow for various emotional expressions, so long as violent or suicidal acts are not permitted to seem heroic.*

To the extent that an atmosphere of "truce and solidarity" emerges, educators should seize the opportunity and build upon it. Collective grieving following a suicide can be a time to open the channels of communication in troubling areas which seldom are discussed. It can be a time to put nagging grievances between groups to rest. It can be a time to renegotiate some of the rules of conduct which have been a source of tension within the school. Most important, it can be a time to reach out to those students who are in crisis and in need of help.

To further promote feelings of solidarity in the face of loss, many experts recommend that educators encourage student participation in appropriate mourning rituals such as memorial services. Such rituals are culturally accepted ways of expressing sorrow and loss; they can help to shape the perceptions and behaviors of the group in a positive way. Any ceremony sanctioned by the school should function to provide a positive outlet for grief, without increasing tensions or romanticizing violence or suicide. The purpose of such rituals should be clear: they give students and staff permission to talk openly about the loss, and they are an opportunity for the living to say goodbye to someone who has perished.

Rituals can be a healthy start to collective grief resolution, so long as students participate voluntarily and are under the surveillance of adults who can help them. *It is inappropriate to force students to participate in a mourning ritual if it is against their wishes or religious beliefs.* Mourning rituals should be an option, but each student's right to participate should be respected.

There is an important note of caution regarding collective grieving to which educators should be sensitive. Collective feelings of loss among students can evolve into a tendency for them to stigmatize and scapegoat. The group's need to find an explanation for senseless death can change into a need to affix blame. This usually happens when educators are themselves poorly prepared to deal with the event, perhaps because of a lack of training and postvention planning. *To the extent that educators appear to their students as confused, insensitive, or not able to communicate with them about what has happened, the tendency to scapegoat will increase.* Finding a scapegoat usually complicates the process of grief recovery by interjecting into the equation negative feelings of anger or hostility.

Educators also should know that not all students will feel a serious loss following the suicide of a peer or teacher. For many students, the initial shock is soon followed by "business as usual." For these students, special programming beyond the school's postvention protocol is not necessary.

Because not everyone feels a deep loss, educators should expect that some students will exhibit a morbid sense of humor by making tasteless jokes. Such jokes have shock value and are a way for some students to show their peers that they are unaffected by the events. Unfortunately, those who are deeply affected are hurt by such disrespect. Educators should anticipate these reactions and strongly discourage morbid humor. They should acknowledge that not everyone will feel the same degree of loss, but each has a duty to respect the grief of another.

In addition, educators should avoid reinforcing in their classrooms certain common misunderstandings and cliches about grief. One such cliche is that "time heals all wounds." Indeed, generation after generation has come to believe that time alone constitutes a magical potion that will somehow lessen deep feelings of loss. The problem is that simply "giving it time" does not necessarily resolve conflicts or alter the conditions which produced the sense of grief.

If educators tell students that *only* time will heal feelings of grief, then they are unintentionally reinforcing in students feelings of powerlessness and hopelessness. This in turn may raise the risk of contagion. Such "folk wisdom" conveys the message that nothing one does will relieve the pain, that one is ultimately alone in suffering, and that inaction (i.e., waiting) rather than action is the single best response to deep sorrow.

Another bit of bad advice regarding grief recovery is when educators tell their students that they "shouldn't think about it" or "shouldn't feel that way." Implied here are several unfortunate messages. Telling grieving students not to dwell on the suicidal death of a classmate translates into telling them to ignore or to bury powerful feelings. Suppressing or ignoring true feelings does not produce a sense of resolution, nor does it result in an emotional state which encourages each student to get on with his or her life in a way that is healthy. Furthermore, telling students not to feel a certain way denies them the right to their feelings. It also implies that they are somehow inadequate for not rationally controlling their emotions.

Such messages can produce three unfortunate consequences. First, some grieving students may begin to experience guilt for feeling (or not feeling) a certain way. This can add to their distress as they reflect on their past relationship with the deceased person (e.g., "I should have told him I loved him," or "We shouldn't have treated her that way.").

Second, students learn to become very guarded in expressing to others how they truly feel out of fear of judgment, censorship, or rejection. When the need for honest communication with others is most critical, grieving students may feel unable to talk about what they are going through. Healthy resolution of the collective grief brought on by the suicide of a classmate is best accomplished in a climate of open communication.

Finally, encouraging students to bury their emotions only serves to confuse them about their true feelings. Collective recovery from a loss usually emerges when each student is honest with self and others, and when each is truly in touch with his or her feelings. Denial, guilt, anger, and an inability to share feelings with others at school is a recipe for prolonging the anguish and for limiting growth potential.

There are two additional bits of folk wisdom which educators should dismiss because they encourage students in a state of grief to deny or suppress feelings. The first is to tell students to "keep busy," regardless of how trivial the task. Immersion into mundane activities does not magically cause those in a state of grief to "snap out of it." Temporary distractions are just that . . . temporary; they often serve to avoid or prolong coming to terms with the loss. Engaging in work, hobbies, or other activities while grieving has value to a point, so long as it does not result in isolation from sources of support or in foregoing efforts to address one's feelings. (The same is true when a person attempts to suppress grief by medicating himself or herself into oblivion.)

The second piece of folk wisdom suggests that a loss can be overcome by acquiring something new. An example of this is a parent telling a child whose pet has died, ". . . not to worry, you will be okay, we'll get you a new one." The obvious problem is that grief is seldom offset by new possessions, nor do new relationships automatically supplant the loss of a loved one. Although well-intentioned, suggesting that something new will somehow lessen or replace the loss may be interpreted by students as a denigration of the deceased. It may also be seen as a crass attempt to buy off their sense of grief, to silence them, and to get them to behave as if everything is back to normal. Little wonder that many grieving students learn to publicly act as if they are fine, while continuing to suffer alone without coming to terms with the loss.

The problem of "acting recovered" is especially common among adolescent students. Often these grieving students neither want to "burden" others (especially their teachers) with their feelings, nor do they want to risk being rejected because others do not know how to respond to their expressions of grief. In a sense, both the griever and others "put on a happy face" and engage in a "conspiracy of silence" to avoid confronting true feelings. This is what John James and Frank Cherry call "Academy Award Recovery" in their book, *The Grief Recovery Handbook* (1988). They aptly state:

". . . the vast majority of verbal and nonverbal communications a griever will hear are appeals to the intellect and do not encourage the expression of feelings. Such intellectualizing actually increases the griever's sense of isolation instead of having the intended result of reducing it. It creates a feeling of being judged, evaluated, and advised. In a relatively short time, the griever discovers that he or she must actually 'ACT recovered' in order to be treated in an acceptable manner."

Because most people find it difficult to know how to respond to another's loss, it becomes a simple thing for all concerned to avoid the subject entirely. Educators should not make this mistake. Complex feelings among students of denial, guilt, anger, confusion, and fear are likely to be compounded by a "conspiracy of silence." Such silence can promote among students an unhealthy sense of isolation from sources of help, and ultimately impair their competencies to act in a healthy manner. That is why school personnel dealing with those students most affected by a peer's death need to understand a basic fact: grief recovery is best accomplished with the help of others rather than alone.

James and Cherry (1988) argue that it is critical to have available someone with whom grieving persons can share feelings in an atmosphere of complete trust and confidentiality. They also suggest that those who grieve write a letter to the deceased, confronting the things that were said and done (or not said and done) in the relationship, and then read the letter to a trusted person who is helping in the process of grief resolution. Furthermore, we suggest that an entire class be given the option of writing a letter of condolence to the family. Students can also be encouraged to write about their feelings in a journal which need not be shared with the teacher or others. These efforts help students to let go, to say goodbye, to make amends, and to gain perspective. Such perspective is the basis for recovery and growth.

According to James and Cherry (1988), "Recovery means claiming your circumstances instead of your circumstances claiming your happiness." Recovery also means being able to hold fond memories without "persistent painful feelings of loss, guilt, regret, or remorse." They also warn against the dangers of "enshrinement" where one "obsessively builds memorials to the person who has died." Finally, recovery is the ability to "forgive others when they say or do things that you know are based on their lack of knowledge about grief." For educators, an important confirmation of recovery occurs if students are able to use their own loss to help others successfully cope with grief.

To help students individually and collectively handle their grief, it is important that educators understand those characteristics of some adolescents which can produce problems in grief resolution. These include:

- lack of an "emotional vocabulary" which allows for the understanding and expression of complex feelings;

- immersion into a sybaritic or pleasure-oriented value system which defines emotional or other pain as unacceptable;

- lack of understanding about the time-limited and treatable nature of depression;

- limited opportunity to publicly mourn in an environment where one can find support;

- self-medication with alcohol or drugs as a means of coping with pain;

- a limited family or peer support system;

- ineffectual problem-solving skills, coupled with limited experience of death;

- immersion into a social network which encourages denial and scapegoating;

- heightened susceptibility to mass media portrayals of violence and death which fail to instruct about the realities of grief and loss.

Educators can enhance the prospects of healthy *collective* grief resolution by anticipating these problems and acting *before* a tragedy occurs. Educators should strive to:

- make issues of death and grief resolution part of the regular health and social studies curriculum in both elementary and secondary schools;

- develop positive peer support systems, including student support groups and peer helping programs;

- model problem-solving skills in the classroom by "thinking aloud" about alternative solutions and their consequences;

- talk with students about death and dying issues as they occur naturally within the context of instruction;

- create opportunities to teach students an emotional vocabulary which empowers them to understand and appropriately express complex feelings;

- encourage students to discuss and rethink those values which promote denial of feelings, intolerance of pain, scapegoating, instant solutions, and an excessive search for pleasure;

- help students to critically examine the content of violent movies and television shows — programming which ignores the consequences of such acts;

- promote a school and peer culture which discourages the use of alcohol or drugs as a means of solving problems or managing stress;

- provide staff training in grief resolution;

- ensure that school libraries develop age-appropriate materials which can help students deal positively with loss;

- create opportunities for appropriate public expressions of grief in a supportive climate following a traumatic event.

With these observations in mind, it is clear that educators should strive to keep open the lines of communication with students and with each other before and after a tragedy. Furthermore, in order to serve as models in helping students cope with loss, educators must first clarify their own feelings and beliefs about death. If discomfort with this topic is addressed before a tragedy, then the ability to communicate with students improves in the wake of a crisis. Armed with the knowledge and skills to help resolve collective feelings of grief, educators can reduce the risk of contagion and can more effectively begin the task of rebuilding a sense of community.

REBUILDING COMMUNITY

Closely related to feelings of grief due to personal loss are feelings of loss of a different nature. One seriously debilitating outcome of death by suicide (especially if the person was popular) is a sense of "lost community." This means that for some students, their personal trauma may be compounded by a feeling that the school community itself is no longer viable. For them, the seriousness and dramatic suddenness of the event undermines the bonds that attach them to other members of the community.

Feelings of lost community following a suicide often translate into numbness, confusion, and even apathy. For most students, such feelings are temporary; they occur in the immediate aftermath of the traumatic event. Yet an important consequence of this sense of lost community is that some students (and faculty) are too stunned to act.

They are unable to effectively coordinate their actions with others in ways which allow them to get on with their lives.* And the very condition of their inaction reinforces in them a sense of alienation — a sense that they are alone, that they are powerless, that their world is unsafe and uncaring, and that there is no one to turn to for help.

Ironically, the confusion and isolation which often accompany feelings of lost community produce an opportunity for educators to improve the school climate. Before a tragedy, some members of the school may already feel alienated. Anti-social rather than altruistic behaviors reflect this felt alienation. Often in school there are status distinctions and unresolved conflicts which undermine feelings of common purpose and limit the willingness of groups to cooperate. For many students, there may be little motivation to share in the continuity of school life.

Tragic events, if properly handled by educators, can provide a context to resolve past conflicts and to affirm the bonds of community membership. Such events provide an opportunity to renegotiate the character of how people relate to one another. School officials should capitalize upon this by doing several interrelated things. First, in all communications to students, parents and others, educators must emphasize that "we are all in this together." In other words, they need to promote an *"esprit de corps"* by setting aside prior conflicts and compartmentalized concerns. The pronouns "we," "our," and "us" should be used to promote unity of purpose.

Appendix D offers guidelines for helping to debrief students and faculty most affected by a tragedy. The same debriefing technique can be used with crisis team members who may feel overwhelmed by the stress of a traumatic event.

Second, in acknowledging that all are affected by the tragedy, it is important to communicate that each member of the community can and should be expected to help. In other words, a sense of altruism should be emphasized as a shared community standard. School officials can promote altruism by making school facilities, staff and resources available to those in need. School staff and other assets should be seen as public resources which are readily accessible to the community. Altruistic behavior also is enhanced if school officials are themselves seen as tirelessly pitching in, if no one is seen as gaining personally at the expense of another, and if it is seen that ever increasing numbers of people are part of some common helping effort. Students in particular should be encouraged to put aside past conflicts and divisiveness in order to help each other when tragedy strikes.

Third, educators can take the lead in rebuilding a sense of community by making sure that everyone who is willing has a task to do in the helping effort. All volunteers should be welcome. This means that before a suicide occurs, a list of needs and tasks should be in place to direct helping efforts. For example, assigning students (and their parents) to distributing literature, raising charitable contributions, or doing other benevolent tasks reinforces the feeling that members of the community have the power to act. Generous praise should be given to all in order to motivate them and to promote pride in their ability to work cooperatively toward regenerative goals.

Fourth, an excellent way to create and to rebuild a sense of community is to establish a peer assistance program. Such programs generate support networks among students who are estranged; they also identify student leaders who model behavior for others.

Fifth, schools should reassess practices which tend to undermine the sense of community. In particular, ability grouping is known to be a source of divisiveness both among students, and between students and teachers. Ability grouping destroys community solidarity to the extent that it reinforces feelings of superiority and inferiority, of status distinctions, of group antagonism, and of "us against them." If such a climate prevails, then developing a sense of common purpose and altruism is made much more difficult.

Finally, when the school is able to resume normal routines despite the tragedy, it serves as a powerful symbol that it is still viable. On the other hand, if there are lengthy delays in returning to the business of education, then the sense of membership in a healthy and vital community is diminished. When the school community is not seen as viable, the competencies of students to learn and to be productive are undermined.

Therefore in the wake of a tragedy, the task of every educator is to rebuild the social bonds of community. Taking action is empowering; shock, confusion, and apathy are reduced by the leadership of school officials. If schools act as a consistent and stabilizing force following a tragedy, then the resiliency of students, parents, and others is enhanced. The sense of lost community can be overcome when the lines of communication remain open, when the school serves as a conduit for information and services, when educators take the lead in promoting altruistic behaviors, and when the task of educating our young — despite the tragedy — returns as the primary focus of school activity.

11
THE SCHOOL'S ROLE IN PRIMARY PREVENTION

Most often what is called primary prevention education is really designed to raise general awareness rather than to prevent the basic conditions which give rise to problems.* A primary prevention program, however, should be more than merely awareness education. While awareness of a problem is important, awareness alone does not translate into effective prevention. Indeed, schools are replete with examples of well-intended sex and drug education programs which fail to prevent teenage pregnancy or drug abuse. They may temporarily raise awareness, but they fail to prevent undesirable behavior because they do little to change certain attributes of the individual or the environment.

At present, most school programs to prevent suicide focus on secondary prevention (often referred to as crisis intervention) and on postvention (McIntosh, 1993). Yet in

---

*Caplan (1964) was the first to differentiate between three levels of prevention: primary, secondary, and tertiary. With respect to suicide, primary prevention activities are designed to reduce the likelihood of a problem ever developing. Secondary prevention refers to timely interventions directed toward those at high risk. Tertiary prevention is postvention programming intended to reduce risk for survivors.

the long run, the most cost effective approach for educators is primary prevention which reduces the number of students who will eventually become suicidal. Although crisis intervention with students known to be at high risk of suicide is important, primary prevention which reduces the number of students who will eventually become suicidal is essential.

We believe that the best approach to suicide prevention is for the schools to develop comprehensive programming which parallels a public health model (see Figure 1). The main objective of such a primary prevention model is to significantly reduce or eliminate the incidence of self-destructive behaviors among students. This objective can be accomplished if schools successfully do two things simultaneously.

First, educators must work to develop in students knowledge, attitudes, and skills which reduce vulnerabilities and promote competencies, especially in relation to optimal mental health. This effort is akin to an inoculation program through its emphasis on building individual competencies to resist unhealthy choices. Second, educators must work to modify the environment in which students function in order to increase their chances of positive, adaptive behaviors. In part, this effort is directed to reducing environmentally induced stress, while increasing positive opportunities.

By emphasizing both competence building and environmental modification, a public health approach recognizes a fundamental condition: youth suicide is linked to student development, especially in terms of how young people learn to cope with stress. In recognizing this fact, however, several questions are raised. Given that all young people face developmental challenges, does this mean that

Figure 1 – Public Health Model of Comprehensive School-based Suicide Prevention Programming

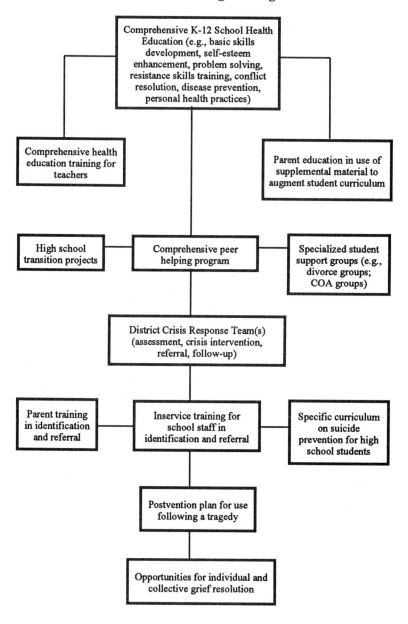

all should be exposed to suicide prevention programming? Should the target population for prevention programming be limited only to those students who may be at demonstrably higher risk of developing suicidal thoughts and behaviors?   Should the focus of programming be specific to concerns over suicide, or should it include a broad range of developmentally damaging behaviors and conditions? Because students vary in their developmental levels, at what point is a suicide prevention program developmentally appropriate? Do schools have sufficient resources and knowledge to address the complexities of competence building and environmental modification basic to suicide prevention?

We believe that the best way to answer these complex questions is to offer a step-by-step guide to effective suicide prevention programming, accompanied by a rationale for each step. The first step is to briefly identify what we know will *not* be an effective suicide prevention effort.

What Does Not Work?

Persons interested in developing effective suicide prevention programs in schools can learn from the mistakes made in other prevention programs.   Substance abuse prevention programming is replete with useful examples of what educators should avoid.   Our review of these programs suggests twelve basic lessons for educators to consider:

1.   Scare tactics seldom deter students from making unhealthy choices (e.g., drug experimentation), especially as students enter adolescence.

2.   School efforts alone, independent of linkages to community organizations, seldom are effective.

3.   Community agencies alone, without a close working relationship with educators, cannot effectively impact on most young people. At best, they usually are limited to working with those already identified as being at high risk.

4.   "One shot" instructional approaches (e.g., occasional films or guest speakers) fail to prevent problems.

5.   Prevention education which begins only in the later years (e.g., in high school rather than in elementary school) seldom works to inhibit undesirable conduct.

6.   Increasing awareness levels about a problem, without fostering skill development to cope with that problem, does little as a form of prevention.

7.   Attempting to address the problem without regard to family or peer networks of students will be ineffective.

8.   Programs to prevent one problem (e.g., substance abuse) usually are ineffective if they are not linked to other related problems (e.g., academic failure, low self-esteem, marginal social skills).

9.   School programs which expose only a limited number of students (rather than all) to prevention messages tend to be ineffective.

10. School programs which do not identify and help students at highest risk will do little to prevent their problematic behaviors.

11. Prevention programs that are the responsibility of a single staff person, rather than a shared responsibility within the school, nearly always fail.

12. Ignoring the problem, or insisting that a particular school is immune to it, will never prevent that problem.

What Should Schools Do?

To these twelve lessons, we add another which is a precondition for any program to be successful. Simply stated, the school must commit sufficient resources to the program in order to ensure that it will be sustained over time. This means a commitment to ongoing inservice training, providing staff with curricular and related resources, and a clear commitment by the school administration to make the program a priority.

An important guiding premise of a successful suicide prevention program is that students are capable of handling age-appropriate information about human problems, including problems which may lead to self-destruction. To keep students ignorant of these problems is tantamount to keeping them vulnerable. Often the difficulty with presenting such information is not the inability of students to understand, but the discomfort that adults have with truthfully communicating the facts to children.

Of course, how and what adults communicate depends upon the age and maturity of the students. A public health approach to suicide prevention education should therefore distinguish between age levels within the school system. At each level, the program should emphasize competence building, instilling certain knowledge and values, and appropriate environmental modification.

SCHOOL PROGRAMMING FOR PUBLIC HEALTH

To be effective, a public health model for schools must begin early. We believe that there are three basic elements of effective primary prevention that must start in the elementary school years, and be reinforced in subsequent years. First, foster in students the basic skills and intellectual competencies necessary for school achievement. A firm foundation in this regard is essential for helping students to build self-confidence and to avoid failure — concerns directly linked to suicide in adolescence. Because educators seek to do this anyway, few would see it as part of suicide prevention programming. Yet the acquisition of intellectual and social agility in the early years (or the lack thereof) is fundamental to whether many of the traumas students face will culminate in suicide. For most students, a sense of intellectual competency is the antithesis of hopelessness.

Second, fostering in students a value system which connects them to others — what social scientists refer to as the social bond — is a form of basic prevention. Arguably, the cohesion of society is linked to the cohesion of its basic units such as families, schools, and communities. When people are estranged from one another, and when families, schools, and communities are unable to be havens of support, individuals — even those with considerable intellectual competencies — have no one to whom they can turn in times of personal crisis. When this happens, the negative social forces acting upon a person's life produce in them a profound sense of social isolation. While it is true that schools alone cannot alter disorganizing social forces such as poverty, urban decay, and the deterioration of families, they can work to foster in students positive social relationships, and simultaneously instill in them values which strengthen social bonds.

The core values associated with altruism, cooperation, non-violence, mutual respect, and personal responsibility — all of which are aspects of good citizenship — are the very things which reduce estrangements and help bond people to one another. These values foster healthy social contact and reinforce feelings of hope amidst personal crises. Such values counter the conditions which give rise to self-destructive impulses. Equally important, creating a support network can change for the better the way people relate to one another at home, work, or school. This in turn can mitigate the stresses imposed by social forces which cleave and divide. In this sense, changing the value climate is a form of environmental modification essential to basic prevention.

The third element of basic prevention is more controversial. This component of prevention education encourages schools to honestly present students with information about human problems, even in the primary grades. Physical and sexual abuse, alcoholism, drug abuse, divorce, interpersonal violence, mental disorders, family conflicts, single parenthood, and a raft of other problems are very real in the lives of students of all ages. They experience such problems in their homes, their neighborhoods, on television, and at school. It is simplistic to believe that the early school years are a time of innocence which require adults to keep students ignorant in order to protect them. Ignorance does not protect students; it harms them. Knowing about the nature of human problems and how best to cope is a sound form of protection.

But how should educators begin to present such complex information to young students? Does this require changing the curriculum in ways which will compete with teaching the basics?

Fortunately, many schools are already adopting curricula designed to reduce "at-risk" behaviors among both elementary and secondary school students (see description of the Michigan Model for Comprehensive School Health Education in *Chapter 12*). These curricula include topics such as substance abuse, child abuse, family conflicts, death, and the complexities of human sexual behaviors. Also included here are peer helping programs which extend the resource network available to students. From these efforts, we have learned that it is best if educators consistently integrate information on human problems into regular coursework such as social studies, language arts, health, and science classes. Educators can build the foundation for primary prevention, including suicide prevention, by addressing human problems in regular classes, and by good counseling and peer assistance programs. To do this successfully, it is essential to begin early.

The Early Grades

In the early elementary school years (grades kindergarten – 3), students begin to realize that the world poses very real dangers to them and to those they love.

Prior to this time, young children are disposed toward fantasy oriented or "magical thinking" about what to do when things go wrong. They gradually learn, however, that bad things happen and that these things do not change by simply wishing them away. As a result, they develop very real fears. They also tend to believe that their actions are what cause bad things to happen (e.g., causing parents to get divorced; causing parents to abuse them). Knowing this about elementary school students points the way for educators to develop appropriate curriculum.

At this age, the curriculum should focus on teaching students at least four basic things:

☆ **First, the curriculum should help students to identify behaviors which are abusive, violent, degrading, harmful, or otherwise disrespectful toward self and others. These younger students especially need to recognize when someone is exploiting them or is using others for selfish reasons.**

☆ **Second, the curriculum should instruct students in how to resist being exploited whenever possible, and more importantly, how to find help for self or others when there is a need.**

☆ **Third, the curriculum should emphasize the rudiments of problem solving (e.g., that behaviors have consequences, that students can decide to change behavior in light of consequences).**

☆ **Fourth, the curriculum should work to build self-esteem, which in turn fosters confidence and a sense of personal power. Part of this effort is to reduce self-blame in cases where one is being victimized.**

This final point — the importance of building self-esteem in young children — cannot be overemphasized. There is an abundance of research which links self-esteem to the social development of children. It is also linked to their academic and other school achievements. Feelings of self-esteem form the basis of students' beliefs about their competencies and worthiness — about whether they believe they can and will learn what is expected, and about their perceived value to others if they succeed or fail.

These beliefs about competence and worth are implicated in the kinds of coping skills and decisions students make as they mature. These include decisions about whether to use drugs, to be abusive toward others, to drop out of school, to enter into relationships where one is used, to run away, and to engage in acts of self-destruction. A curriculum which promotes in all students self-esteem, feelings of being of value to others, competency skills, and respect for the rights and integrity of others is the basis of creating a belief that there is hope for the future.

The Middle Grades

Effective prevention curriculum in grades 4 – 8 has "competency enhancement" as the chief goal. This curriculum should build upon the basic knowledge, values, and skills established in the earlier grades. The emphasis is on gradually fostering in students a range of positive social skills which allow them to cope with the ever more complex network of social arrangements in which they find themselves. Specifically, there are four broad yet interrelated components included in this curriculum: interpersonal problem solving skills, decision making, resistance skills training, and empowerment.

Interpersonal problem solving involves taking others into account as one seeks to accomplish a particular end. Decision making may or may not involve others as one ponders a range of options. Both interpersonal problem solving and decision making skills are just that — skills. They can be acquired through direct experience, and they can be learned through instruction. The goal is to systematically expose students, in a controlled environment, to real life problems that they may encounter in school, at home, among peers, and elsewhere. Following such exposure, the objective is to help them explore solutions by modeling for them appropriate responses, and by discussing with them alternative lines of action and their consequences. It is important that students understand two fundamental concepts: they always have choices when facing a problem, and the choices they make will determine the extent to which that problem is solved or grows worse.

In addition, students need to acquire resistance skills as part of their competency enhancement. One central component of these resistance skills is learning to cope with the demands, pressures, stresses, and conflicts that emerge in the context of their peer affiliations. Learning to get along, to mediate conflicts, to reject inappropriate demands, to respect the rights of others, and to continue to feel positive about self even when one chooses not to give in to negative peer pressures are important elements implicated in the acquisition of resistance skills. It is also important that students learn to generalize these skills to other contexts, including negative media influences and inappropriate demands from family members.

When taken together, problem solving skills, decision making, and resistance skills serve as the background conditions of personal empowerment. Personal

empowerment includes these acquired skills, but is more
than their sum total.   Empowerment is a cognitive state
wherein people enter situations with the premise that they
are in control of their lives, that they can act rather than
only be acted upon, and that they have the ability to make a
difference.   It is an outgrowth of first having developed
healthy self-images.   In a sense, personal empowerment
means believing in one's capabilities, and giving one's self
the authority to take appropriate action and to be the master
of one's fate.

The importance of students acquiring a sense of
empowerment is central to effective prevention
programming, especially suicide prevention.   A sense of
empowerment stands as a counterpoint to feelings of
futility and hopelessness that accompany the suicidal state.
To empower with knowledge, skills, and values is to give
one a sense of hope — a sense that one can endure
adversity because one has the power and ability to prevail.
If hope is the belief that things will be better, empowerment
is the realization that one can develop a plan of action to
bring about those desired outcomes.   Perhaps the single
most powerful deterrent to suicide is to create in students a
sense of hope in the possibilities of a better future, and to
give them the tools to act toward the realization of that
future.   That is empowerment.

The High School Years

Building upon the foundation established in the earlier
years, older students (grades 9 – 12) should be exposed to a
focused curriculum with two broad yet interrelated
objectives.   The first objective is to teach all students to
recognize when their peers (and their family members as
well) are at risk of serious harm, including the risk of

self-destruction. To do this means that educators must raise the issue of self-destruction (and other health risks) with students. Talking around the issue by using euphemisms and vague generalities will not suffice. The issue of self-destruction must be addressed head on, with specific emphasis on symptom recognition. While some may consider this to be controversial, such an approach is defensible in the context of a public health model. We already know that the alternative — keeping students ignorant of the problem — is worse. We believe that the need to teach all students to recognize suicide warning signs is analogous to teaching them about AIDS: both are a matter of life or death.

In addition to teaching students to recognize in their peers warning signs of danger, educators must also teach students referral skills. As a public health effort, students need to know what help is available for specific problems, and how to seek that help. They also need to learn about issues of confidentiality (e.g., it is never appropriate to keep a secret that a peer is planning to commit suicide), about how to approach peers who might be in need, and about their own limitations and responsibilities in trying to provide help.

Because the risk of self-destructive behavior increases as students enter adolescence, because the peer network becomes an increasingly important source of influence in the lives of students, and because peers are often the first to learn of a classmate's problems, we are left with a simple conclusion: we must educate all students to be gatekeepers for health. Empowering peers to recognize and to refer friends at risk, coupled with empowering them with the knowledge, values, and skills to make healthy personal choices, is the essence of a public health approach to prevention.

Increasing the Chances of Success

The success of a public health approach to primary prevention can be enhanced if schools adhere to several additional principles. For example, even though all students should be exposed to prevention programming, certain groups of students who are known to be at potentially high risk for developing unhealthy behaviors should be given special attention, if deemed appropriate. These may include those known to have been physically or sexually abused, students who are having difficulty coping with their parents' divorce, children of alcoholics, students who are social isolates, students with very low self-esteem, or others whose circumstances require attention. If there is any indication that their needs are going unmet, offering them individualized attention can be beneficial. Often this can be done in the context of peer assisted social skills training or other forms of outreach (e.g., home visitation) which serve as adjuncts to the basic prevention program. It can also be done as part of a program offering specialized student support groups.

Another principle which follows a public health approach entails how prevention information is presented to students. Again we emphasize that the idea is to start "inoculating" students with prevention messages at an early age, and then give "booster" sessions throughout their school years. These messages should be given in "small doses" when they are young, and as their knowledge base or "tolerance" for the information increases, the information should be presented in more "concentrated" form. This tends to produce beneficial long term changes that would not occur with a "one shot" approach. The objective is to expose students gradually by integrating the knowledge, skills, and values associated with healthy lifestyles throughout the curriculum. Such an approach will help students to build up their "resistance" so that they may cope more effectively.

In addition, basic prevention efforts are more likely to succeed if educators consider ways to enhance the credibility of their messages to students. For example, it is wise to be sensitive to issues of racial and cultural diversity, as well as to the lifestyles of students. Often prevention messages are more credible if the information includes examples which reflect such diversity. Furthermore, if those presenting information are of the same racial or ethnic background as the students, the message credibility may be enhanced.

It is also critical that those presenting prevention messages are themselves healthy individuals who will be seen by students as role models for desirable conduct. Employing trained students to present prevention information, especially to younger students, often will reinforce the messages presented by adults.

Finally, the credibility of the message is increased if the educators are perceived as knowledgeable by students. This requires a commitment to training educators in the use of appropriate prevention curricula.

When taken together, competence building, instilling appropriate knowledge and values, fostering healthy self-images, and working to strengthen the social bond, should form the basis of all prevention efforts, including suicide prevention. Such efforts should not be controversial in the sense that most people would agree that these are desirable objectives. Unfortunately, however, schools seldom have accomplished these objectives to their fullest. Too many students fail to acquire needed knowledge, values and skills at the elementary level, and consequently their problems grow exponentially as they mature. They simply lack the foundation necessary to help them cope with pain and to believe that their future is hopeful.

The conclusion to be drawn is clear. Unless educators are given the resources and training to instill in all students these critical competencies and values, the risks young people face, including the risk that hopelessness imposes, will not diminish. More and more of our young will be threatened, as will the fabric and stability of our society.

IS SUICIDE PREVENTION PROGRAMMING POTENTIALLY DANGEROUS?

The challenge of preventing students from taking their own lives generates heated debate among educators and health care providers. Questions abound. Should schools offer programs which will attempt to prevent suicide among students? If suicide prevention education is offered in schools, will it be safe? Who should be the target of suicide prevention programming, and who should present such programs in the schools? Can schools effectively devote resources to all aspects of suicide prevention? Do we really know enough about what does and does not work in preventing youth suicide to offer a coherent strategy?

Because suicide prevention programming in school settings is relatively new, there is little solid evaluative data to answer unequivocally all such questions. The situation is somewhat analogous to the early 1970's when child abuse programs were first being introduced into the schools. Educators worked in concert with human service professionals, developing rational program models with sensible goals, which reflected a growing understanding of the seriousness of child abuse. Fortunately, lack of experience in offering abuse prevention education did not deter educators from taking the initiative in developing programs. Their need to act was imperative, reflecting the increasing legislative and public pressure on schools to respond, and perhaps more importantly, reflecting sincere commitment to helping improve the lives of their students.

The same rationale applies to the need for schools to engage in suicide prevention education. The problem of youth suicide is so great that both public pressure and professional ethics dictate school involvement. True, it would be ideal to have an extensive battery of program evaluation research to guide school practices. Yet we must start somewhere, and the experience of the many educators, clinicians and others who have grappled with the issue of youth suicide suggests that successful prevention programs can and should be implemented.

As knowledge of what works increases, programs should be modified accordingly. But currently we know enough for our schools to take several steps. And the very first step is to quell the concerns of those who claim that suicide prevention programming in schools is at best ineffective, and at worst, potentially dangerous.

One issue in the debate over the possible dangers of suicide prevention programs in school centers on the role of suggestion in affecting suicidal behavior. Some argue that talking about suicide to students might put thoughts of self-destruction into their heads. This view contends that for vulnerable persons, simply talking about suicide — even in a preventative sense — is suggestive and may unintentionally increase the number of suicide attempts, threats and gestures among those needing to gain attention. At the very least, some fear that talking about suicide to students desensitizes them to such a horrific act, thus reducing their inhibitions toward self-destruction.

It is the view of many experts, however, that by discussing suicide in an honest and open fashion, and by placing emphasis on prevention, the risk of self-destruction among students will be lowered. Preliminary research supports this view. In an early study, for example, Barrett (1985) found that after training in suicide prevention, students reported increased knowledge of warning signs and felt more confident about how to help their high-risk friends. Importantly, no suicides occurred in those schools where such prevention programming was provided.

Similarly, the California State Department of Education (1987b) reported that following a five hour suicide prevention curriculum, high school students demonstrated an improved capacity to respond appropriately to a suicidal crisis. Students showed increased knowledge of warning signs, intervention techniques, and resources for getting help. Ninety percent of the students surveyed expressed strong approval of suicide prevention education in the schools. Twenty-six percent of the students indicated they were somewhat uncomfortable with the topic, but thought it was an important subject to discuss anyway.

But does increased knowledge translate into effective action? One year after classroom instruction, researchers for the California State Department of Education surveyed 420 students in five high schools who participated in pilot testing of curriculum materials. Twenty-two percent of the students responded that as a result of the program, they had been able to prevent one or more suicides or suicide attempts.

In related studies, Ross (1985) found that following training, students do refer themselves and others for intervention. In fact, the number of students requesting help for themselves or their friends at a suicide prevention center following training at school increased over 250 percent (from 166 students seeking services to 437 students). Gryphon Place (1992) in Kalamazoo, Michigan, found that following a five hour suicide prevention curriculum for 1398 high school students, an average of 1.8 students per class (average class size = 20.3) referred themselves or were referred by others for mental health intervention.

Despite some of these promising studies, the argument over the appropriateness of student training in suicide prevention continues. Recent research has added even more heat to the debate. For example, in 1991 newspaper and television stories in the United States and Canada reported in rather sensationalistic fashion that school-based suicide prevention programs may be dangerous to students. These media accounts reflected the concerns raised by a team of researchers who had published their findings in the prestigious Journal of the American Medical Association (Shaffer, Vieland, Garland, Rojas, Underwood & Busner, 1990). Specifically, the researchers reported that following exposure to suicide prevention programming, "high-risk" students (those who had previously attempted suicide) showed no positive change in their deviant attitudes toward self-destruction. In addition, it was reported that attempters exposed to the prevention program were less likely than low-risk students to recommend that the program be repeated for others. They were also more likely to believe that discussing suicide in the classroom could be risky.

This research, accompanied by sensationalistic media accounts, added fuel to those fanning the flames of resistance to suicide prevention education in schools. For those opposed to such programming, the perceived dangers, coupled with the lack of school resources to handle such a complex problem, led them to conclude that the task of prevention should reside exclusively with the mental health profession and not with the schools. Apparently they believe that educators simply are not capable of competently educating students in ways which will prevent suicide.

But does the research support such a view? Might this view justify schools doing nothing to address a growing problem? Are the claims overstated that suicide prevention programming in schools is dangerous?

From our assessment of the problem, we find no compelling evidence to support the conclusion that properly developed school-based suicide prevention programs are dangerous. Indeed, we believe that the real danger is if schools fail to act to stem the tide of self-destructive behaviors among our young. While there is need for caution in instituting such programs, the research simply does not warrant the conclusion that schools offering suicide prevention education are acting in a reckless and dangerous fashion.

Furthermore, the research by Shaffer and associates (1990) regarding the presumed danger of suicide prevention programming in schools is seriously flawed.

Their research was conducted on only two school-based suicide prevention programs out of the hundreds that exist. The two prevention programs selected for study were extremely limited in focus. The two programs were only one-to-three hours in length. More comprehensive programs which were available for study were not chosen for assessment. In addition, the study relied on a highly dubious instrument — a self-report questionnaire with low reliability. Many students changed their responses on an important control question from pre-to-post-testing (Tierney & Lang, 1991).

Their study had other serious limitations as well. According to Tierney and Lang (1991), the study did not measure whether high risk students experienced increased suicidal feelings or behaviors after the program; it only measured whether these students thought others might be upset by the program. Tierney and Lang also point out that the study failed to ask whether suicide attempters were more or less likely to use helping resources following exposure to the program. These are important omissions.

To these observations, we add others. The questionnaire only sought to measure student attitudes; it did not attempt to measure behavioral changes among either low or high risk groups as a result of exposure to the prevention program. The negative conclusions of the study were derived primarily from a small subgroup of respondents. In general, this group of suicide attempters reported somewhat negative attitudes toward the prevention program. Yet such a finding is not surprising for an obvious reason: a program which functions to openly confront students with the inappropriateness of dysfunctional suicidal thoughts and behaviors is likely to seem threatening to some who have attempted self-destruction. These students, especially if they are suffering from psychological impairment, are unlikely to enjoy having to face their shortcomings (Clark, 1991). It is not surprising that some high risk students held negative attitudes toward the prevention program. It is noteworthy, however, that this group did not report any *new* suicidal behaviors that could be linked to the program.

Can we conclude from the study by Shaffer and his colleagues that suicide prevention programming in school is dangerous? In this particular study, there was no evidence that prevention education made those who attempted suicide or other students *more* prone to take their own lives. Thus far, the hundreds of other prevention programs have yet to reveal any evidence that this form of education is harmful. To the contrary, even the study by Shaffer and associates found that the majority of respondents — those who had never attempted suicide — showed no negative reactions to the program. Indeed, many may have increased their understanding of the problem and of where to find help — two important prevention goals. Equally important, because peers are most often in the best position to know of a classmate's plans to commit suicide, it is especially valuable for these peers to learn how to identify problems, and to learn about how and where to find help. The study, however, never attempted to measure whether students in the program were better able to recognize suicide risk in classmates or to seek appropriate help.

Unfortunately, Shaffer et al. (1990) never offered either the basic principles or a detailed prescription for schools to follow in order to develop effective primary prevention. They concluded that the prevention programs examined were not effective because they failed to change the pathological behaviors (which were never actually measured) of those who were most psychologically disturbed.

This confuses a prevention program with a mental health treatment program. A primary prevention program in school is not and should not serve as a form of clinical treatment for those at highest risk. As we have argued, students needing clinical intervention should be screened and referred to mental health professionals. Screening is an important prevention goal for those at high risk. But more importantly, the main emphasis of primary prevention in school should be to instill in all students the knowledge, values and skills which reduce the likelihood of self-destruction or other health-compromising behaviors.

We agree with many experts (Berman, 1987, 1991; Felner, 1990; Kalafat & Elias, 1991; Kalafat & Ryerson, 1989; Poland, 1989; Ryerson, 1987b; Smith, Eyeman, Dyck, & Ryerson, 1988; Tierney, Ramsay, Tanney & Lang, 1991) that better evaluation of suicide prevention curricula for students is important, particularly the examination of behavioral outcomes (e.g., changes in the number of students seeking help for at-risk friends or themselves; reduction in attempts and completions). Yet we believe that there is enough evidence to demonstrate that educating peers about warning signs, and educating them about sources of help for at-risk friends, are valuable components of an effective primary prevention curriculum.

12
IMPLEMENTING PRIMARY PREVENTION CURRICULA

We have argued that a public health approach to suicide prevention entails the use of a comprehensive school health curriculum. At the elementary and middle school levels, this curriculum should emphasize acquisition of basic skills, respect for self and others, problem solving, resistance skills, and empowerment. At the high school level, the curriculum should build upon these skills and go on to emphasize instruction specific to suicide, including symptom recognition, referral skills, and stress management.

There are several key elements in developing a suicide-specific curriculum at the high school level. There are several key elements in developing a suicide prevention curriculum at the high school level. First, it is crucial to have a trained crisis response team and teaching staff in place before training students. From experience, we know that there is an increase in referrals for suicide and other risk following student training. Referrals come from teachers, peers, and the students themselves. The crisis response team should be given advanced notice of the student training so they can plan for the anticipated increase in referrals.

Second, school professionals targeted to teach this material should be carefully selected. They should be warm, caring, approachable, credible, and stable educators with a strong sense of optimism. No educator should be forced to teach this material. Those selected to teach the curriculum should hold the attitude that suicide is preventable and that teaching others to intervene is important.

Third, staff members expected to teach the curriculum should receive sufficient inservice training, either by members of the crisis response team, or by a mental health professional. The trainer should have both expertise in suicide prevention, as well as familiarity with the curriculum to be used. Inservice training should accomplish the following objectives.

- Increase teachers' knowledge and skill in suicide prevention and intervention.

- Inform teachers about community resources, including direct services to students and their families.

- Allow teachers to explore their own attitudes and beliefs about suicide prior to instructing students.

- Enhance teachers' ability to talk candidly about the topic without feeling discomfort.

- Help teachers to effectively use the curriculum in instructing their students.

Fourth, as suggested by the California State Department of Education (1987a), it is best if each class is team-taught. With two presenters, one staff member can teach the material, while the other is free to observe students' reactions and provide help to students who appear to be upset. A crisis response team member who is already familiar with the material is an ideal co-leader; she or he may even want to take the lead in teaching the material, particularly the first time it is offered. Having two professionals team-teach the curriculum can provide more opportunities for mutual support, peer consultation, and peer supervision. Most often teachers will need release time to consult with co-leaders and to plan the lessons.

Fifth, the material should be taught as early in the day as possible so that referrals can be handled immediately. For similar reasons, the curriculum should not be taught the week before a vacation (Ruof, Harris, & Robbie, 1987).

Sixth, decide in advance whether the school will obtain parent permission for student participation in the curriculum. While some schools ask for written permission from parents before teaching the suicide prevention curriculum, most schools do not require such permission. For example, school districts in California are not required to secure parental permission, and schools in Wisconsin simply send notification to parents about the curriculum, but do not obtain written permission. Like Poland (1989), we do not advocate obtaining written permission from parents for each student's participation. Schools may be setting themselves up for only partial participation if written permission is a prerequisite. Parents who do not want their child exposed to the material can request to have him or her excluded.

Nevertheless, there should always be written information sent to parents about the curriculum in advance of the student training. If possible, it is best to offer suicide prevention training to parents first. For those parents who still have questions or concerns, an individual meeting with their child's teacher might be scheduled.

Finally, decide when the material should be presented to students. Building upon the components of primary prevention implied in a public health approach, we believe that students benefit most from specific suicide prevention education during their first year of senior high school. Suicide rates for students younger than fourteen are very low, but begin increasing significantly once students reach high school. Younger students do not always have the cognitive maturity to comprehend the complexities of the material. As previously discussed, the focus of training prior to senior high school should be more generic: coping with stress, problem solving skills, academic and social skills development, enhancing self-esteem, and empowering students with the values and knowledge to make good decisions.

Components of a Suicide Prevention Curriculum

We stress again that the best approach to a suicide prevention curriculum for adolescents follows a public health model. There are three broad yet interrelated objectives to such a model. First, students must recognize when friends and family members are at serious risk for self-destruction. Teaching students to recognize suicidal warning signs is analogous to teaching them about sexually transmitted diseases. Such knowledge may save a life.

Second, students must know where help is available for those at risk, and they must learn how to access that help. Included here are the limitations and responsibilities for students seeking to help their peers.

Third, positive coping strategies and problem solving skills should be emphasized. Empowering students with the knowledge, values, and skills to make healthy personal choices — and to model those healthy choices for their peers — is a crucial part of a public health approach to prevention.

To accomplish these broad objectives, a suicide prevention curriculum for high school students should include the following components.

- Dispelling erroneous beliefs about suicide, such as: (1) asking about suicidal intent directly puts ideas into people's heads; (2) friends who talk about suicide seldom mean it; (3) truly suicidal people give no warning signs; (4) you can't really stop a person if they are serious about suicide.

- Clarifying what is involved in a suicidal crisis (e.g., hopelessness and the erosion of coping skills, as well as the relationship between substance abuse, depression, and suicide).

- Recognizing suicide (or other crisis) warning signs.

- Learning how to ask if a friend is in imminent danger (e.g., "Are you thinking of suicide?" "Do you have a plan?" "Have you ever attempted suicide before?").

- Understanding how to communicate effectively with a friend who is considering suicide (e.g., listen for and accept feelings; show support and caring; offer hope that alternatives are available; do not minimize the problem or moralize).

- Discussing the limits of confidentiality and responsibility (e.g., emphasize that it is never appropriate to keep someone's suicidal thinking a secret; let students know that their role is to get help for their friend and not to act as a counselor).

- Explaining how to get adult help for those at risk (e.g., how to tell a suicidal friend that the information cannot be kept confidential; what to do if the first adult approached for help does not respond appropriately; identify available school and community resources and how to access these resources).

- Considering healthy alternatives to suicide (e.g., understanding that depression is temporary and treatable; explaining how to cope constructively with stress or negative life events; differentiating between suicidal thoughts and suicidal actions so students see that thinking about it does not mean one must act on that impulse).

- Empowering students by letting them know: (1) the time-limited and situational nature of suicidal thinking; (2) the ambivalence of most troubled students about the choice of suicide; (3) that the vast majority of adolescent suicides are preventable; and (4) that one caring person can usually make a difference in whether high-risk peers seek help.

Usually five hours is the minimum amount of time needed to teach students the above components. Periodic review of these basic ideas is also important. A number of commercially available suicide prevention curricula for students are described in depth in *Appendix E.* Most of these curricula are five hours in length and can be incorporated into a variety of subject areas. These include but are not limited to Health, Social Studies, Family Living, Consumer Education, Psychology, Sociology, and Home Economics. Some schools have even incorporated the curriculum into English and other classes.

Suicide prevention education should be a top priority for inclusion in the high school health curriculum. One potential obstacle to student training is the lack of time to include the lessons in an already crowded schedule. In some cases, adopting a suicide prevention curriculum may mean that other lessons get consolidated or dropped. However, most schools can be more creative in adopting the curriculum. For example, schools may wish to consider teaching one or more prevention objectives in English, Social Studies, or other appropriate courses. It might also be helpful to use some "study hall" time — time which is often wasted by students — to implement part of the program. We believe that adding just a few hours of suicide prevention education to the existing curriculum can result in a tremendous pay off — saved lives.

Guidelines for Teachers

The California State Department of Education (1987a) and Poland (1989) outline a number of suggestions for school professionals responsible for teaching a suicide prevention curriculum. The following are many of their suggestions, as well as our own.

Warning signs, intervention skills, referral strategies, and ways to cope productively with depression or other problems should form the foundation of any suicide prevention curriculum used with students.

All audiovisual materials should be screened to ensure that warning signs and intervention skills are emphasized. Graphic films or those that unintentionally sensationalize or romanticize suicide should be avoided (e.g., those that: (1) depict a suicide or suicide attempt; (2) show teenagers with lethal instruments; (3) discuss specific methods). Following a video or filmstrip, students should be encouraged to assess the film's realism, as well as discuss both the warning signs and the actions taken by others to prevent suicide. Regardless of whether videos are used, avoid doing anything to sensationalize suicide while teaching the material (e.g., discussing detailed methods of suicide, taking a trip to the morgue or cemetery, asking an attempter to "tell their story").

Use the term "we" rather than "you" as much as possible in presenting the curriculum. In teaching their curriculum, the California State Department of Education (1987a) found that using "we" suggests a common experience and a shared vision, while "you" can sometimes sound condescending or imply judgment (e.g., "There are certain signs we might notice when we suspect our friends are feeling down.").

Be sensitive to the responses of students known to have had family or other loved ones commit suicide. Teachers should approach these students privately and allow them to decide the level of participation at which they would feel most comfortable. If a student reveals the suicide of a loved one once the curriculum is underway, teachers should attempt to assess the curriculum's impact and allow the student to be excluded if appropriate. If such students find the material upsetting, they should be referred to a member of the crisis response team to talk about their feelings and be assessed for possible risk.

Carefully attend to all students' responses as the curriculum is presented. Students who look visibly upset, who withdraw from discussion or participation, who seem unduly preoccupied with a particular issue, who ask questions that seem unusual, who continually crack jokes or who appear angry or hostile, should be approached privately to determine if a referral to the counselor's office or crisis response team is appropriate. In addition, all students who reveal a past attempt or continuing suicidal ideation should be referred as well.

If there have been previous suicides at the school, acknowledge them in a caring way, but do not share details as a way to illustrate a point. Keep case examples hypothetical without reference to suicidal methods.

Let students know at the beginning that they will not be expected to share in class private information about themselves or family members. Some students with poor interpersonal judgment may try to share information that is best left confidential. Teachers should make every effort to protect students' privacy and to ensure that peers do not obtain information that could result in teasing or rejection.

Make an effort to keep the atmosphere positive. Selected use of humor is appropriate to relieve stress or to reduce the intensity of the material. Inspire optimism that better solutions are always available and that students can make a difference with seriously troubled friends by helping them to seek adult assistance.

If students will be involved in role play, make it voluntary and make it safe. The California State Department of Education (1987a) has outlined useful guidelines for conducting role play within the context of a suicide prevention curriculum. For example, they suggest setting the scene and the parameters in advance, and helping students distance themselves from their roles by using props such as glasses, hats, articles of clothing, and sports equipment which remind both the observers and role players that they are distinct from the roles they play. Students who participate in role plays should be called by their real names before the class is dismissed. If students appear uncomfortable playing the role of the suicidal student, an adult should volunteer to play it.

Do not force students to participate in large group discussions, small group exercises, or role play activities. Allow each student to determine the degree of their participation. For example, in their implementation of a state-wide curriculum, the California State Department of Education (1987a) emphasized the importance of teachers' awareness and respect for cultural differences in students' responses to the material. Minority youth, including Hispanics, Asians, and Native Americans may be more private about their feelings on this topic than others.

Let students know each day which adults are available to talk with them individually about questions or concerns, and how they can access these professionals. Ideally, at least one professional should be available to meet with students after class. In addition, be knowledgeable of available community resources for students who may need immediate referral to a professional outside the school.

Carefully review students' responses to paper and pencil activities each day for signs of hopelessness, serious depression, or suicidal thinking. Refer these students to a member of the crisis response team for risk assessment. If students select suicide as a research topic, guide their writing so that it emphasizes prevention, problem solving, and stress management. In addition, end each day's lesson on an upbeat note that sends a message of empowerment (e.g., "With your help, we can make a difference in preventing teen suicide." "Suicide is preventable, and tomorrow we're going to talk about ways we can help a friend who is thinking of suicide." "There are always better solutions to problems than suicide, and this week we will be talking about ways to cope when we're feeling down.").

Know the limits of your role in advance. For most educators, this involves providing information, support, concern, and referral linkages to others more qualified to intervene directly with suicidal students. A teacher should not be expected to function as a therapist.

In addition to promoting competencies and empowering students to make healthy personal choices, suicide prevention also involves modifying the environment in which students function. A public health approach to suicide prevention strives to reduce environmentally induced stress in school. High school transition projects are a powerful form of environmental modification which can lower the risk of maladaptive behaviors in students.

HIGH SCHOOL
TRANSITION PROJECTS

Students experiencing major life transitions can be vulnerable to psychological and behavioral difficulties. For some, the transitions from elementary to junior high school, and from junior to senior high school, are accompanied by significant declines in academic performance, attendance, and self-esteem, with concomitant increases in depression, anxiety, problem behavior such as substance abuse, unprotected sexual activity, and delinquency.* In extreme cases, these adaptive difficulties can initiate a downward spiral that ends in suicide.

Many educators and therapists note that the organization and climate of high school can increase maladjustment problems for vulnerable new students. Incoming students must adjust to a new physical environment, a large number of peers whom they do not know, new teachers and staff, and new sets of rules and expectations. Teachers and school staff also are expected to address the needs of a mass of new students whom they do not yet know. Not surprisingly, those new students experiencing serious adjustment problems may simply be overlooked. As such, schools would benefit from rethinking some of their past practices in order to better meet the needs of students in transition.

---

*For a more thorough review of this issue, the following research is helpful: (Blyth, Simmons, & Carlton-Ford, 1983; Felner & Adan, 1988; Felner, Ginter, & Primavera, 1982; Felner, Primavera, & Cauce, 1981; Gilchrist, Schinke, Snow, Schilling, & Senechal, 1988; Hirsch & Rapkin, 1987; Simmons, Burgeson, Carlton-Ford, & Blyth, 1987).

A Case Illustration

To combat problems of transition, Felner and his associates (Felner & Adan, 1988; Felner, Ginter, & Primavera, 1982) designed a multi-element primary prevention program to reduce the degree of complexity and confusion in a new school setting, as well as increase sources of social support from teachers and peers. The program can be applied in junior or senior high schools in which entering students come from two or more feeder schools. While the program benefits all students, the researchers found it was of particular benefit to students with limited coping skills and few sources of support. These are the very students most at risk for suicide.

The program had two primary components: restructuring the role of homeroom teachers, and reorganizing the school environment to facilitate the establishment of a stable peer support system. In this program, homeroom teachers were assigned to a class of new students. Roles were redefined so that homeroom teachers acted as the primary administrative and counseling link between the students, their parents, and the rest of the school.

Many of the responsibilities usually carried out by guidance counselors and other school personnel were then performed by homeroom teachers. For example, homeroom teachers aided their cohort of students with such tasks as selecting classes, assisting with both school-related and personal difficulties, and providing information about school rules and expectations. In addition, each student was seen individually by the homeroom teacher for at least 15-20 minutes once every 4-5 weeks.

When a student was absent, the homeroom teacher, rather than other school personnel, contacted the family and followed up on excuses. Prior to the beginning of the school year, homeroom teachers contacted the parents of incoming new students to explain their role and to encourage these parents to call or come in if they had questions or concerns.

The intent of these changes was to increase the amount of academic and social support students received from teachers, to decrease students' sense of anonymity, to increase students' feelings of accountability, and to assist students in accessing school rules.

Teachers participating in the program received one day of training on basic listening skills, early identification of emotional and academic difficulties, strategies for helping students cope, suggestions for raising concerns with parents, and referral procedures for troubled students. A second day of training was devoted to team-building, enhancing communication among teachers, clarifying program expectations and roles, and arriving at consensus about team meeting times. It was emphasized that the goal was to enhance available support to students, not for teachers to replace school mental health staff. Counselors, social workers, and other support personnel also participated in the second day of training. Training occurred before the start of the school year.

Once the program was underway, teachers received consultation and supervision from school guidance staff about how to carry out their new roles. In addition, project teachers met briefly as a group, once or twice per week, to identify students needing additional help or support from guidance personnel. Students for whom a family contact was needed were also identified.

The second component of the prevention program created by Felner and his associates entailed a partial reorganization of the school's social system. Incoming students were assigned to classes in their four primary academic subjects (English, Mathematics, Social Studies, and Science) with the same group of students. This modification reduced a common problem — a constantly shifting peer group in each of the classes across the school day. Participating in homeroom, and at least four classes with the same group of students, provided a high degree of overlap and consistency.

In addition, project classrooms were located in close proximity to one another. Minimizing distances between classes facilitated students' sense of familiarity with the school, and offered more opportunity for informal interaction among classmates. It also reduced the need for young students to pass through parts of the building in which there were older students. This physical arrangement reduced (at least for a time) young students' exposure to difficult social pressures from older students. The purpose was to facilitate the development of peer support, enhance the students' sense of belonging, and foster perceptions of the school as a stable, understandable, cohesive, and well-organized place.

The research results reported by Felner and his associates indicated that program participants had significantly less absenteeism in ninth grade than students who did not participate in the project (an average of 9 days difference between groups). Although program and control students had almost identical eighth grade GPA's, by the end of ninth grade, the program students had significantly higher GPA's than did students in the control group (2.78 and 2.29 respectively). Furthermore, a long-term follow-up of students in the program found that their drop-out rate was less than half of the rate for students in the control group.

Program and control students were given mid-year and end-of-year self-concept measures. Scores revealed that program students' self-conceptions generally remained stable, while control group students showed marked declines during the school year. Students were also given an instrument measuring their views about the school's social climate during the middle and end of ninth grade. Students in the program reported significantly more positive feelings about their school environment than did control group students. Those who participated in the prevention program reported substantially higher levels of teacher support and involvement, and a sense of being in a more growth-enhancing social climate.

An unexpected result of the program was increased satisfaction with teaching for participating teachers. Teachers reported being less overwhelmed by the demands posed by entering students, and more able to influence students. They also felt more connected to their students.

In summary, Felner and his colleagues demonstrated that changes in the roles of school personnel, as well as changes in the school's social environment, can prevent academic and personal difficulties associated with school transitions. Such a program may well provide increased opportunities for school personnel to recognize students at risk for suicide and other health-compromising behaviors. Additional positive features of the program include the low cost, potential for improving teacher morale, and the minimal disruption of instruction.

Despite the merits of this one demonstration project, however, it is clear that schools need an even more comprehensive approach to combat the range of health risks to students. We believe that the most comprehensive approach to date — an approach which is being implemented state-wide and which is a model for other states to follow — is in Michigan.

MICHIGAN'S HEALTH EDUCATION PROGRAM

In 1983, five different state agencies in Michigan proposed the establishment of a single comprehensive school health education curriculum. The goal was to provide a consistent and comprehensive curriculum to all school-age children in the areas of mental and physical health. The curriculum was designed to develop in children, at an early age, the skills, knowledge, and attitudes necessary to reduce health risk, including reducing behaviors which contribute to the risk of self-destruction.

The proposal was accepted and became an important component of the Governor's Health Care Cost Containment program. Legislative endorsement and appropriations followed acceptance of the proposal by the Governor. Early in 1984, three validated comprehensive school health education curricula and other material were merged to form the "Michigan Model for Comprehensive School Health Education." The intent was to use the best features of existing curricula and to coordinate federal, state, and local resources behind one curriculum. This comprehensive curriculum was seen as the best vehicle for delivering new health information to teachers and students as it became available (Michigan Model State Steering Committee, 1991).

The Michigan Model curriculum consists of approximately 40 lessons at each grade level K-8. It covers ten topic areas which include: disease prevention and control, personal health practices, nutrition, growth and development, family health, substance abuse, consumer health, safety and first-aid, community health, and emotional and mental health. Life skill competencies, including decision making and problem solving, resisting peer pressure, stress management, success orientation, and self-esteem enhancement are important elements of the curriculum. Topics are introduced, expanded upon, and reinforced at age-appropriate grade levels to ensure a strong scope and sequence. Because health education information can change, ongoing curriculum committees periodically update the material to include new content.

Each teacher implementing the curriculum attends 30 hours of health education training. This training provides teachers with current health information, as well as training in the use of materials and activities. Teacher manuals are supplemented with health education materials that promote "hands-on" learning. Models, charts, A-V resources, books, and structured activities help students to be involved in the curriculum. As the curriculum is revised, teachers receive 4-6 hours of retraining to review updated information and new teaching methods.

Each grade level has an accompanying parent manual. These manuals contain information on what students are learning in class, along with suggestions and activities for reinforcing classroom instruction at home. Resource lists are provided, and feedback forms are included for parents to communicate their feelings about the curriculum.

The Michigan Model began implementation during the 1984-85 school year in 34 public school districts. By the 1992-93 school year, 446 out of 525 public school districts (85%) and 129 private schools were participating. Almost 800,000 students in grades K-8 (72% of K-8 students enrolled in public schools) were receiving the curriculum. To date, the Michigan Model is the largest comprehensive school-based health education program in the country.

The program is coordinated by a statewide steering committee. State agencies represented on the committee include: the Department of Education (lead agency for implementation), the Departments of Mental Health, Public Health, Social Services, State Police, and the Office of Substance Abuse Services. A Michigan Model Coordinator from each of the 26 regions across the state provides local coordination of the curriculum. Each regional coordinator acts as liaison between local school districts, classroom teachers, community resource agencies and personnel, in-service trainers, and the Department of Education. Coordinators also facilitate local steering committees consisting of representatives from government, health agencies, and school personnel. Local health professionals and agencies assist with teacher training. The multi-agency networking at both the local and state level gives the Michigan Model a broad base of support.

The program is funded cooperatively by both public and private sources. State and federal appropriations provide most of the funding. A twenty percent local match comprised of public and private resources is provided by participating districts. Local steering committees help in locating private support.

The Michigan Model is one of the outstanding models of health education currently available in North America. Among the superior features are its clear and comprehensive scope and sequence of skills from kindergarten to eighth grade, the systematic presentation of health information in numerous areas of importance, and the integration of coping skills, stress management, and problem solving into health instruction.

Preliminary research on its effectiveness demonstrates a reduction in health-compromising behaviors for participating children, as well as an increase in health-promoting behaviors. In a nonrandom survey of nearly 5000 parents, those responding reported the following changes in their children's behavior: increased use of seatbelts, increased tooth brushing, increased physical exercise and eating healthier snacks, increased traffic and safety rule compliance, and increased knowledge about the dangers of tobacco, alcohol, and other drugs (Michigan Model State Steering Committee, 1991).

In a study conducted by the University of Michigan (Shope, Marcoux, & Thompson, 1989), 6th and 7th grade students who participated in the substance abuse prevention portion of the curriculum used significantly less tobacco, alcohol, and marijuana than students not exposed to the lessons at a one year follow-up posttest. Participating students also demonstrated better understanding of the risks of tobacco, alcohol, and other drugs, a keener awareness of the pressures placed on students to use these substances, and more knowledge of how to resist these pressures than students who did not receive the lessons.

In 1987, the Michigan Model was recognized as one of the twenty most effective programs in substance abuse prevention by the National Association of State Alcohol and Drug Abuse Directors in cooperation with the National Prevention Network and the Federal Office for Substance Abuse Prevention. The Michigan Model is often featured at national conferences as an exemplary school health initiative, including the American School Health Association and American Public Health Association's annual conferences. In 1992, it was highlighted as a model program in a report on school-based health promotion by the Harvard School of Public Health (Lavin, Shapiro, & Weill, 1992).

The next objective is to phase in comprehensive school health education instruction to all of Michigan's K-12 population, including students in private schools. Plans are also underway to develop a 9-12 grade curriculum, a preschool curriculum, and a curriculum adapted to the special needs of handicapped children.

Although the long-term outcomes of this curriculum are as yet unknown, the Michigan Model does reflect a well-conceived and comprehensive public health approach to prevention. It avoids repeating the mistake of seeking a "quick fix" to the many health risks facing students. It systematically works to instill in all students the knowledge, values, and skills necessary for healthy choices.

From our perspective, the conclusion is obvious: a comprehensive school-based approach to health education — one which starts early, builds skills, enhances knowledge and healthy values, and one which includes messages about preventing suicide — will save lives and improve the quality of life for students and their families.

13
CREATING PEER
ASSISTANCE PROGRAMS

A student's peers are often the first to know if he or she is experiencing a personal crisis, including a suicidal crisis. In a national survey conducted by the Gallup Organization (1991), 77% of the students questioned stated that if they were contemplating suicide, they would first turn to a friend for help.

Across the United States and Canada, many schools are capitalizing upon this already existing system of peer-to-peer interaction. These schools are initiating programs to train students to help their peers in coping with problems. Such programming has become so popular in recent years that it constitutes a significant movement within education. Students trained in these programs have gone by a variety of names such as peer helpers, peer assistant leaders, peer facilitators, peer listeners, peer resources, peer tutors, and peer educators.

Support for this trend is reflected in a large body of research* demonstrating the effectiveness of training stu-

---

*(We refer the reader to research on peer helpers conducted by the following: Botvin, Baker, Renick, Filazzola, & Botvin, 1984; Bowman, 1982; Bowman & Myrick, 1987; Huey, 1985; Hoover, 1984; Johnson, 1978; Luepker, Johnson, & Murphy, 1983; Maher & Christopher, 1982; McEvoy & McEvoy, 1991; Mitchell, McGee, & Tompkins, 1985; Murphy, 1975; Myrick & Bowman, 1981a; Samuels & Samuels, 1975; Telch, Kellen, & McAlister, 1982; Tindall, 1979; Tobler, 1986.)

dents to serve in a helping capacity. This research high-lights the value of peer helpers in improving their fellow students' classroom behavior, school attendance, attitudes, achievement levels, self-esteem, and adjustments to high school. This research also shows that peer helpers can be valuable in lowering substance abuse among younger students, and in reducing discipline referrals at school. Peer assistance programs can enhance school climate and be a valuable adjunct to school-based prevention and intervention efforts.

A driving force in these burgeoning peer assistance programs is the need to increase the number of helping resources for at-risk youth. The reality of educational budgets means that schools often cannot hire enough support personnel, thus making it difficult to meet all the counseling and guidance needs of students. Compounding the problem of staff shortages are the often excessive administrative responsibilities of support staff (e.g., arranging students' class schedules; committee work). Such duties limit the time available to see students in a helping capacity. Peer leaders, therefore, provide one cost-effective way of providing needed support to at-risk students who might otherwise "fall through the cracks" if left to seek help on their own.

There are many potential benefits of a school-based peer helping program. By empowering students to be responsible for each other, schools can increase social and academic assistance, as well as early identification, intervention, and appropriate referral of at-risk students.

Peer helpers can also serve as powerful role models of problem solving and positive coping behaviors. By promoting healthy behavior, peer leaders are an important element in developing a positive peer culture and healthier school climate. For example, in evaluating one county-wide peer helpers program, school administrators reported fewer crisis situations following the program's implementation (McEvoy & LeClaire, 1993). There also were fewer problematic student behaviors such as poor attitude, truancy, discipline referrals, and absenteeism.

Although the long-term effects of peer assistance programs have yet to be fully assessed, initial research suggests another benefit. The peer helpers make as many, if not more, gains in personal growth as the students with whom they work (Bowman & Myrick, 1980; McEvoy & LeClaire, 1993; Myrick & Bowman, 1981a).

Peer assistance programs are by no means a panacea. Many schools, however, are embracing peer assistance programs because they have the potential to prevent not only student suicide, but to reduce a range of related negative behaviors (e.g., academic failure, dropping out, substance abuse, and teen pregnancy). Recognition of this potential is reflected not only in the increasing number of schools developing peer helping programs, but also in the availability of federal, state, and local funding for such efforts.

But caution is in order. Peer helping programs cannot be effective if they exist in the absence of comprehensive school policies and programs to address the range of risk conditions facing students. Moreover, peer helping programs are no substitute for student access to a professionally trained staff. Therefore, educators need to know how to develop, implement, and evaluate such programs as part of the school's comprehensive effort to prevent youth suicide and related risks.

THE PEER ASSISTANT
LEADERSHIP (PALS) PROGRAM

To illustrate what educators can do, we have selected a model peer assistance program as a case study. Similar to other programs, a series of tragedies sparked its creation.

During a fifteen week period in 1984, Paw Paw High School in Paw Paw, Michigan experienced three suicides and two serious suicide attempts. Students were aware of the details surrounding these events, and were deeply affected by them. In response to community-wide fear concerning the "contagion factor," a Community Planning Committee (CPC) was formed. Representatives on the committee included school administrators, community mental health workers, the police chief, ministers, substance abuse professionals, and parents. The CPC immediately sought funding for activities aimed at containing further contagion (e.g., inservice training on crisis intervention, pocket-sized cards with emergency numbers for students, survivors of suicide groups). Although these activities were helpful, committee members and others felt that a long-range plan for preventing adolescent depression and suicide, as well as related problems, was essential.

Van Buren County Community Mental Health, in collaboration with the CPC, wrote a state grant that was funded by the Michigan Department of Mental Health Prevention Services. The grant was for the 1986-87 school year, and included as one of its key components a school-based peer assistance program in Paw Paw High School. The grant supported a full time therapist from Community Mental Health to assist in the development, implementation, and supervision of the program.

In the years since its inception, the Peer Assistant Leadership (PAL) Program has expanded to eight school districts in Van Buren County. It has also spread to five school districts in neighboring Allegan County. It was there that seven student suicides, in a six month period in 1987, prompted the development of a comprehensive suicide prevention program with peer helping as a central component. The PAL program has received state and national recognition as a model of school and agency collaboration in suicide prevention and intervention. Using this model, the following is a step-by-step guide for developing, implementing, and evaluating a peer helping program in schools.

I. PLANNING PHASE

Lead time of one year is necessary in order to conduct the advanced planning required to develop a comprehensive peer helping program. It is essential that enough time be allowed for the following: conduct a needs assessment; research exemplary programs; build a support base; clarify responsibilities related to staffing and financing; develop and approve a training curriculum; recruit trainees early enough to allow for inclusion of the class in their course schedules; and obtain a physical space for the program. The following is a detailed description of each of these steps.

Needs Assessment

The first step is conducting a needs assessment. Information obtained from interviewing administrators, teaching staff, students, and parents can be used to support the need for the program, guide the development of program goals, and determine how peer leaders can best be used. In Allegan County, for example, needs assessment data resulted in some schools emphasizing conflict mediation in PAL training, while others focused on tutoring or other skills.

Building Program Support

Building administrative and faculty support for peer helping can be accomplished in a number of ways. First, information from a needs assessment should demonstrate the necessity of the program. Potential direct benefits should be emphasized (e.g., fewer discipline referrals, fewer students in crisis, better attendance, improved school climate).

Second, administrators, teaching staff, students, and parents should be invited to provide recommendations at every step in the planning process. Some schools have formed a planning committee consisting of school, parent, and community representatives whose task it is to provide ongoing consultation, resources, and support for the program (see *Chapter 14*). Some of these committees have obtained financial resources. In our experience, the more program ownership felt by the school and community, the more support engendered.

Finally, anticipate possible objections to various program components and consider ways to reduce these. For instance, in the PAL program, students use class time to see a peer helper. As a result, there are clear-cut rules as to when and how often students see the peer helper. In addition, teachers are given the power to veto the privilege if it seems inappropriate for the student to leave class (e.g., in the event of a major test or review).

We caution against calling the trained students "peer counselors" because this name is likely to raise objections to the program. Administrative staff, teachers, and parents may feel uncomfortable with the notion of students "counseling" other students. Counseling is often interpreted by others as acting in the role of expert, diagnostician, or therapist. Clearly, students are not clinical experts, nor should they be viewed as such. Using terms such as "peer helpers," "peer assistant leaders," or "peer facilitators" will clarify the role of trainees, and reduce the possibility of program opposition.

Program Structure

The quality, length, and type of training provided to peer leaders is crucial to program success. The format used to provide peer training varies in programs across the country (e.g., class for credit, weekend workshops, seminars in the summer, training after school).

After reviewing a number of programs nationally, Van Buren and Allegan County schools used as their model the Peer Helper Training Manual developed by Houghton and Lemons (1985) for the Fairfax County Schools. Students are trained in an 18 week class for credit.

A class format has many advantages over other options. First, a class for credit allows for comprehensive training of students. Second, it can result in better retention and integration of new skills, and provide opportunities for structured, on-going supervision. Third, it fosters the development of group cohesion among trainees. Finally, it enhances both the credibility and visibility of the program.

Staffing

In Van Buren and Allegan County schools, the PAL class is team-taught. The team includes a certified teacher or counselor at the school who serves as an in-school coordinator, and a community professional (e.g., mental health clinician or substance abuse specialist). The in-school coordinator brings teaching and administrative skills to the program, and acts as the primary liaison to the rest of the school. The community professional provides crisis intervention expertise, guides program development, and facilitates referral to community resources. This team approach enhances not only the skill level of trainees, but it firmly establishes a cooperative relationship between the schools and community service providers.

The role of the two professional staff is to accomplish the following objectives:

- develop the curriculum;

- recruit and train peer helpers;

- provide support, supervision, and back-up to peer leaders;

- handle crisis situations that require professional involvement;

- offer short-term early intervention counseling;

- establish referral to service providers in the community;

- provide training for faculty in the identification of "high risk" students;

- run support groups, where appropriate, for special groups of students (e.g., newcomers to the school, children of divorce);

- promote the program to school personnel and the community.

The selection of professional staff is critical to the success of the program. Communication and problem solving skills, initiative, the capacity for negotiation, and interpersonal skills are as important as educational background in staff selection. It is a recipe to fail if staff are assigned to the program, not out of interest or ability, but rather out of expedience (e.g., they were merely "available" or were "volunteered").

Most schools with a PAL program recruit an in-school coordinator from existing staff. Usually this means reassigning some of the coordinator's existing duties to other personnel. Simply dumping this additional responsibility upon the new coordinator without reducing other duties is likely to doom the program to inattention. If schools are to have an effective program, it will require constant oversight by the coordinator. This cannot be done on the cheap.

The position of the community professional is part-time in some districts and full-time in others, depending upon resources. Although funding for the community professional's position originally came from a grant, the funding base for PAL programs has expanded considerably. Funding sources now include the schools, Michigan Department of Mental Health, Community Mental Health, Regional Substance Abuse Agencies, County Commissioners, United Way, community foundations, local businesses, service clubs, private donations, and school-based fundraisers.

Curriculum Development and Approval

Fortunately, educators can select from already developed curricula to train peer helpers. Resources include materials developed by Akita and Mooney (1982), Foster (1993), Myrick and Bowman (1981b), Myrick and Erney (1984, 1985), Tindall (1989), Tindall and Gray (1988, 1989), and Varenhorst (1980). (For a more extensive list of training resources, see *Appendix F.*)

Program administrators should gear the content of training to reflect the needs assessment data. For example, if a goal is to teach substance abuse resistance skills, trainees must have knowledge of communication techniques, refusal skills, decision-making, and health information. Similarly, if peer helpers are expected to act as group leaders, then training in group facilitation is essential.

Although the content will vary somewhat from school to school, the following are issues to be covered in training:

- attending behaviors (e.g., eye contact, body posture);

- facilitative responding (e.g., recognizing and reflecting others' feelings, clarifying ideas, asking open-ended questions, providing feedback, using confrontation appropriately, knowledge of communication stoppers);

- problem solving (e.g., identifying the problem, brainstorming alternative solutions, evaluating the consequences of each solution, selecting and implementing the new alternative, and evaluating the success of the alternative selected);

- confidentiality (e.g., boundaries and limits of confidentiality, consequences for breaches in confidentiality);

- suicide intervention (e.g., recognizing warning signs, assessment and intervention techniques, referral procedures);

- dynamics of grief/loss (e.g., types of loss, the grieving process, offering support to others);

- examination of social issues affecting adolescents (e.g., child abuse, substance abuse, teen pregnancy, sexually transmitted diseases, and eating disorders);

- referral procedures (e.g., how and when to refer to supervisors, awareness of community resources).

The curriculum might also include training in one or more of the following areas:

- tutoring approaches;

- conflict mediation training;

- group facilitation skills;

- refusal skills training.

If the training is for credit, it must be presented to each school district's curriculum committee and school board for approval and accreditation as an elective.

Selection of Trainees

The next step is the recruitment and selection of peer helpers. In Van Buren and Allegan Counties, each year a school-wide survey is administered which asks students to identify "natural helpers" who they might turn to if they were experiencing personal problems. Students are asked to nominate three peers who show sensitivity, warmth, trustworthiness, acceptance of others, and availability to friends in need.

Nominees are brought together and presented with information about the responsibilities of being a peer helper. Those who wish to participate are asked to obtain two recommendations from teachers, employers, or other unrelated adults, and fill out an application form. The form seeks information about the applicant's motivation, personal strengths, and experiences which might prepare the student for being a peer leader. Motivated students who are not nominated by peers, but who wish to be considered for training, can apply by writing a short autobiography and filling out the requisite forms.

Given the nature of the training, all potential applicants are asked to obtain written parental permission to be involved. Applicants' parents are sent letters explaining the training, program goals, and permission forms. A "Parent's Night" is also held where staff meet with parents of interested students to explain the program and answer questions.

Students who complete the application process are then interviewed individually by the PAL staff. No more than twenty students are selected for the training class.

When a class is larger than twenty, staff often report difficulties in providing effective training and supervision.

High priority is given to recruiting trainees from all social classes within the school, a mixture of males and females, upper and lower classmen, and a racial/ethnic balance. We found that students from "marginal" social groups are uncomfortable seeking out peer helpers chosen solely for their outstanding academic achievement or high standing in "popular" cliques. As a result, natural helpers from a heterogeneous cross section of social groups are selected. Selection of trainees begins in the spring preceding the targeted school year to allow for inclusion of the class in students' fall schedules.

Obtaining Program Space

Space must be reserved in the school for a "peer helping room" to be used exclusively for activities related to the program (e.g., tutoring, support groups, conflict mediation, one-to-one listening). In some schools, it may be a converted classroom. In others, it may be an unused storage area or conference room. Enough room is needed to accommodate both individual and group work with students.

The room can be furnished with used but comfortable sofas, chairs, and tables, as well as a stand with pamphlets covering a range of subjects (e.g., substance abuse, family planning, anorexia, local helping resources). A locked file cabinet should also be made available to secure confidential information.

Forms and Procedures

The final step in planning is the development of procedures for program operation. These include:

- how students should make appointments to see peer facilitators;

- when and how often students can use the peer assistance service, particularly during class time;

- a contact sheet for peer helpers regarding the type of contact made with a student, the referral source, the problem discussed, and the help provided;

- criteria for referring a case to supervisory staff for intervention or follow-up;

- a policy on confidentiality; and

- referral procedures to community service agencies when appropriate (e.g., Community Mental Health, Substance Abuse Agency, Protective Services, Adolescent Health Clinic).

II. IMPLEMENTATION PHASE

Training

In Van Buren and Allegan Counties, the semester-long PAL training begins in the fall of each school year. The content of the training is skill-focused (e.g., listening, facilitative responding, problem solving) rather than focused solely on personal growth. In addition, training is primarily experiential rather than didactic.

Adolescents best learn these types of skills through hands-on activities.

Skills are introduced and modeled for students by the staff. Students then practice in dyads and triads, receiving feedback both from trainers and other trainees. Homework assignments are developed to provide additional practice. Methods for evaluating student progress include videotaped performance of the skills being taught, ratings on teacher, peer, and self-evaluations, tests, research reports on adolescent issues (e.g., pregnancy, suicide), book evaluations, classroom participation, and fulfillment of obligations in assigned group work.

Confidentiality

A key component emphasized with trainees is the nature and importance of confidentiality. Without a sense of trust to communicate openly, students will never use a peer assistance program. Ground rules concerning confidentiality need to be established the first day of training. Trainees should not be allowed to discuss personal issues brought up by others during training without explicit permission. They may, however, be encouraged to share the general activities occurring during training, as well as their own personal reactions to these activities.

Once helpers begin providing services, the supervisors *always* need to be apprised of the nature of the problems being discussed, and have enough information to know when adult intervention is necessary. Peer facilitators must know exactly how to involve supervisory staff, and when professional intervention is needed.

In cases of child abuse and neglect, and those involving imminent danger to a person's life (e.g., suicidal or homicidal threats), supervisors are mandated by law to break confidentiality and report the information to the appropriate agency. Ultimately it is the supervisor who determines which situations demand release of confidential information. Although peer leaders should have a comprehensive knowledge of available community resources to share with students, they should not be allowed to make contact at these agencies for students. If the situation is life-threatening, the supervisor or student's parents make the initial contact with the community agency.

Clear-cut consequences for breaches of confidentiality by peer helpers need to be established. For example, in some schools, breaches result in the immediate suspension of peer leader privileges and responsibilities.

PAL Assignments

After training, most PALS are assigned to placements within the school district. Some are assigned to the PAL room at the high school one hour per day for the school year. At least one PAL is available to high school students every hour of the school day. In some school districts, PALS are also placed in a PAL room in the junior high school. Others have daily placements in the elementary schools. Each assigned PAL receives partial academic credit for his or her placement. This type of credit is similar to that which a library or office aide might receive. PALS placed at the junior high or elementary schools either walk to their placement (if next to the high school) or drive their cars if within a five minute driving distance.

Some PALS are unable to be assigned to a placement following training because of scheduling problems. These trained helpers are referred to as "PALS-At-Large" and make contact with students whenever their services are requested (e.g., before or after school, at lunch breaks). PALS-At-Large do not receive academic credit for their activities as do those with daily placements.

Once trained, PALS serve in a variety of supportive roles. All the PALS participate in group projects such as welcoming transfer students to the school, making community presentations about the program, or sponsoring alcohol-free social events.

Some PALS are paired in buddy arrangements with new students, especially those having difficulty adjusting. PALS help these students get oriented, involve them in school activities, and encourage them in developing new friendships. Others are used to provide accurate information, dispel myths, and allay fears of junior high school students anticipating the move to senior high school. Concerns about peer pressure, substance abuse, and academic expectations typically are addressed.

PALS often serve as peer educators by sharing health information and by modeling skills to resist pressure to smoke and drink. These programs emphasize communication skills, refusal skills, and decision-making as part of a comprehensive substance abuse prevention program. In addition, PALS are used to co-facilitate adolescent support groups (e.g., coping with divorce, newcomers group). Group leaders are PAL supervisors or other school professionals such as the social worker or psychologist. Peer leaders, however, should *never* be given the sole responsibility of directing what might be defined as "group therapy." Whatever their helping task, it must always be under the careful scrutiny of adult supervisors.

PALS assigned to the PAL room at the junior and senior high schools spend most of their time meeting individually with students. These peer leaders offer students tutoring, support, or problem solving assistance.

Students seek PALS for a variety of reasons: problems involving family members, peers, or school staff, concerns about their own or others' substance use, academic problems, loss issues resulting from death, divorce, or termination of romantic relationships, information about birth control and pregnancy, stress, social isolation, depression, and suicidal ideation. Students with high-risk behaviors or complex concerns are immediately referred to the professional staff for further intervention or referral to community agencies.

PALS assigned to the elementary schools often are used as classroom aides or are paired with students experiencing academic difficulties. Tutoring is provided as needed. PALS also act as Big Brothers/Sisters to younger students in need of a caring relationship.

Increasingly, PALS are called upon to engage in conflict mediation with disputing individuals or groups. They act as educators in the art of compromise, negotiation, and reaching a settlement, thus reducing the incidence of hostile exchanges and violence between students. In this regard, peers are often more successful than adult educators in communicating effectively with the factions.

Supervision

Individual and group supervision of peer helpers is critical. Adult supervision should be ongoing both during and following training. Supervision sessions are used to:

- teach new skills and reinforce old ones;

- give support and encouragement as trainees take on new challenges;

- provide feedback on performance;

- reestablish role boundaries for students "helping" in inappropriate ways;

- encourage group cohesion;

- maintain a sense of commitment to the program and its goals;

- plan for future activities.

Without regular supervision and debriefing, peer helpers can become overwhelmed or discouraged in their helping efforts. It is important for supervisors to periodically reemphasize role boundaries with trainees who get overextended by making too many student contacts, or who get overinvolved with students who seek their services. *Supervisors must always be alert to the possibility that a helper is taking on and personalizing the problems of other students. Supervisors must also set firm limits on helpers' attempts to inappropriately "rescue" students, or who assume the role of "expert" and intervene intrusively.*

The frequency and length of supervision depends on the nature and number of projects involving peer helpers. For peer helpers engaged in one-to-one listening activities, at least one supervision session should be scheduled each week. For those acting as classroom aides in the elementary schools where guidance is already provided by the classroom teacher, less frequent formal supervision is appropriate, usually twice a month. PALS-At-Large are usually seen for supervision at least once per month. Group supervision with all peer helpers should occur a minimum of once per month, and can be used to plan future events or new projects.

Informing Students and Parents

Following training, PALS make classroom presentations about the program to all students in participating schools. Guidelines concerning when and how students can use the PAL service, procedures for making appointments, and the confidentiality policy are emphasized in these presentations. The kinds of problems shared with PALS are discussed, and the voluntary nature of the program is also explained.

At the same time, parents of all students are sent a letter informing them of the PAL program and its services. Parents who do not want their child to use the PAL service are asked to return a "refusal of permission" form. In our experience, only a handful of parents in each district refuse to allow their child to see a PAL.

Maintaining Cohesion and Motivation

Following training, many activities can be used to maintain group cohesion and renew motivation. These activities can also serve to showcase services, increase visibility of the program, and provide special recognition for peer helpers. For example, once a week, PALS wear sweatshirts with the program name and logo on them. In addition, the bulletin board outside the PAL room has pictures of the PALS, along with a short biographical sketch. Highlighted on other bulletin boards are the services PALS provide. Other activities include PAL sponsored homecoming floats, dances, pep assemblies, softball tournaments, and pizza parties. Once a year PALS from all over Southwestern Michigan participate in a one day conference. This provides additional training, special recognition, and the opportunity to share program features with PALS from other schools. Future recruiting of peer helpers becomes much easier as a result of these activities.

III. EVALUATION PHASE

Evaluation of the peer helping program is essential. Evaluation data can be used to maintain support, make program changes, secure funding, and expand the program where appropriate. Tindall and Gray (1989) recommend conducting outcome evaluation in three areas: (1) the program's impact on the peer assistants; (2) the effects of the program on students receiving peer helping services; and (3) the projects peer facilitators undertake (e.g., high school transition programs, drop-out prevention projects). To these, we add two other areas of evaluation: (4) the judgments of teachers and staff about the strengths and limitations of the program; and (5) the views of parents whose children are peer leaders.

PAL Program Results: An Illustration

Since the start of the PAL Program in 1986, there has been only one student suicide in the thirteen participating school districts.   Equally important, there has been a dramatic increase in the number of students identified, appropriately referred, and treated for suicide risk. There also has been an increase in the number of adolescents referred to community agencies for other dysfunctional behaviors (e.g., substance abuse, school failure, sexual exploitation).

Comprehensive evaluation of the PAL program was obtained from PALS, administrators, teaching staff, students, and parents of peer helpers (McEvoy & LeClaire, 1993).   Surveys were administered to 8 administrators, 86 high school teachers, 1419 high school students, 43 PALS, and 23 parents of PALS in three school districts in Allegan County.

Positive results were almost immediate.   After only one year, seven out of the eight administrators reported fewer discipline referrals, more crisis situations diffused, and increased tolerance for seeking help at school.   By the second year, 50% of the teachers surveyed stated that the PAL program had already impacted positively on problem behaviors (e.g., poor attitude, truancy, discipline), helped faculty feel better about dealing with problem students, and improved the general school climate.   Almost none of the teaching staff rated the program impact negatively.

During the first five months of PAL service alone, 13% of the students in participating districts used the program.   The number of students using the service has increased each year since the program was established.

Seventy-five percent of the high school students who used the PAL service agreed or strongly agreed that the PAL had helped them to better understand their problems, and had helped them work towards problem resolution. Even when their problem was not school-related, 42% stated that they felt better about school after talking to a PAL.

Less than ten percent of the students who used the PAL service stated they would have felt more comfortable talking to an adult (an option which they still had open to them). Almost ninety percent of the students who met with a PAL said they would see a PAL again if they had a problem.

PALS were asked to rate themselves on a number of interpersonal skills before and after the PAL training. Over ninety percent of the PALS reported greater awareness of their own and others' feelings, had increased awareness of how their behavior affected others, and had a greater ability to listen to others. Eighty-four percent reported an improved ability to communicate with family members after training. Almost ninety percent reported an improved self-concept and a better ability to cope with problems. Self-reported gains in interpersonal skills were corroborated by survey results from parents and teachers. There was an added benefit to the program: the number of school absences decreased and the GPAs increased among the peer assistant leaders. In essence, their leadership role in the PAL program enhanced their capacity to serve as *academic* role models. These results are consistent with others who report that the peer leaders themselves directly benefit from their training and leadership roles.

IV. EXPANSION PHASE

Following the introduction of the PAL program in 1986, almost twenty school districts in a five county area in Southwestern Michigan have adopted the program. Schools in Indiana, Illinois, and Ohio have also implemented PAL services based upon this model.

In 1989, the Michigan Department of Mental Health Prevention Services wrote guidelines for the development of a comprehensive peer helping program using the PAL program as its model. Consultation in the development of a PAL program is currently available from this state agency, as well as from Van Buren and Allegan County Community Mental Health Services, and Allegan County Substance Abuse Agency (see *Appendix F*).

Peer helping programs have led to the formation of fruitful partnerships between local human service agencies and the schools. As a result, agency responsiveness to school referrals and the amount of collaborative case management for at-risk adolescents has increased dramatically. In addition, the development of innovative prevention projects has resulted from such partnerships.

Although the program was developed in a rural area, it is also relevant for urban schools. Of course, the unique features and needs of each school need to be considered when developing peer programming.

A CAUTIONARY NOTE

Despite their obvious advantages, peer assistance programs are no panacea. There is a real danger that some schools, faced with staff shortages and shrinking resources,

will view peer assistance programming as a low cost
substitute for other comprehensive interventions. Such
programming can only be effective if it is but one
component in a school's broad effort to meet prevention
and intervention goals. Effective intervention is not cheap;
peer assistance programs are not "the answer" to staff
shortages, but rather are an important adjunct to existing
programming.

In addition, for peer helping to work, each school
must make a long-term commitment to staffing and
overseeing the program. Normal student turnover
necessitates annual or semi-annual training, as well as
constant adult supervision. A one-shot approach to
training, or allowing students to oversee the program, is an
invitation to disaster.

Finally, the point cannot be stressed too strongly that
vigilant oversight of peer helpers by trained professionals is
essential. There is always the danger that some peer
leaders, in their desire to help, will become so
overwhelmed that they place themselves at risk, or they no
longer function adequately as helpers. Again, careful
monitoring and regular debriefing are essential to protect
the students, and to protect the school from possible
liability.

Despite these caveats, peer assistance programs hold
great promise in the school's effort to reduce health and
safety risks for students, including the risk of suicide. The
fact that they are being adopted widely in the United States
and Canada suggests the obvious: schools are recognizing
that many of their students need help, and they are willing
to try innovative ways to provide that help.

14
UNDERSTANDING THE POLITICS OF COLLABORATION

The problem of youth suicide is, in part, linked to an array of other social problems such as family dysfunction, violence, and substance abuse. Because these are community problems which extend far beyond the boundaries of the school, what can we reasonably expect schools to do to reduce youth suicide? How can we create a common effort to prevent suicide?

The likelihood of creating effective suicide prevention programs is increased if there is genuine collaboration between the schools and community organizations. There is ample evidence which points to the importance of community-wide collaboration; schools simply lack the resources to do it all by themselves. The combined efforts of schools and community agencies is essential if there is to be any hope of reducing suicide and other risks among students. Unfortunately, however, there are often serious barriers to developing an effective working relationship. Yet the need for school-community collaboration as part of a public health approach to suicide prevention is imperative.

We must therefore consider how best to build effective partnerships. Partnerships between schools and community organizations can:

- save schools and agencies money by pooling resources;

- help educators and human service workers to accomplish their tasks more effectively;

- help parents to do a better job of parenting;

- help students to make healthy choices;

- improve service delivery, especially during a crisis;

- improve the quality of community life;

- help prevent the conditions which produce a suicidal crisis.

The good news is that in many communities, successful school-community programs have been launched to address youth suicide and related problems. The bad news is that these often are isolated efforts which are initiated because of the hard work and vision of a single person. In order for a public health approach to youth suicide prevention to become a reality, a coordinated team approach is necessary.

This is easier said than done. The difficulty, in part, is that few educators have learned to view local mental health and other service agencies as educational resources. Likewise, persons working in human services tend to see the tasks of educators as separate from their own. Each seemingly operates in isolated spheres, overlooking common needs and shared problems.

If we know anything about youth suicide it is this: if we fail to build collaborations between education and human services, then problems will get worse. We will be failing our children and ourselves.

Creating Task Forces

Collaboration in the development of prevention and crisis intervention programs, in sharing resources, in exchanging information, and in following through on implementation is possible through the formation of task forces. The ideal task force is one which will unite people who have a vested interested in solving a problem, and who can carry out a plan of action. Among the objectives of the task force might be the following:

- developing and reviewing age appropriate health curricula for all students;

- developing and reviewing a range of crisis intervention measures, including the creation of a school crisis response team or teams;

- establishing a postvention protocol to reduce the risk of contagion, and to guide schools and agencies if a student or teacher suicide occurs;

- training teachers in symptom recognition and referral, and in the use of prevention curricula;

- pooling resources to avoid costly duplication;

- establishing procedures for program evaluation;

- training human service professionals to work with school personnel on educational programs.

Usually task forces are composed of representatives from human services, medicine, education and elsewhere. Sometimes the central school administration takes the initiative in the formation of task forces. In other instances, community leaders or agency representatives assume this leadership role. Regardless of where the primary responsibility for coordination resides, building a broad-based coalition makes sense.

In attempting to build this coalition, however, leaders should understand the obstacles to effective collaboration. Knowledge of the following difficulties can help to reduce potential conflicts which undermine success.

- Be aware that task force members may have conflicting agendas. Issues of turf protection, of division of responsibilities and of program "ownership" can emerge very early.

- Be sensitive to past conflicts between school and agency personnel. Such conflicts are not likely to be forgotten and can undermine confidence in each other. Some may claim that "we are already doing these things," while others question the success of these efforts. As a result, when innovative suggestions are made, some may interpret these suggestions as a vote of "no confidence" regarding what they claim to be doing already.

- Be aware that some task force members will claim expertise in areas where they have little training or experience. For example, having had a close friend commit suicide does not make one an expert on the nature of the problem.

- Be sensitive to the need for all task force representatives to secure a valuable but intangible asset — public recognition. Pride in what one is doing (or has accomplished) should not be seen as unwanted hubris, but as an asset which can be channeled into strong commitment to achieving the task force's goals.

All these potential difficulties share a common theme: communication. If the character of communication between task force members is negative, then there will be little hope of success. The only things likely to be produced are paperwork, cynicism, and finger pointing. This is deadly to creating an effective prevention program. The following is an illustration of these communication problems.

A Case Illustration

Following a rash of suicides among students in an Ohio community, school officials, mental health representatives and other concerned persons formed a task force to find ways to prevent future tragedies. Fortunately, most persons selected for the task force had some background in dealing with student problems, and each had a strong commitment to reducing the risk of student suicide. Unfortunately, however, the leaders who selected the task force were unaware of previous difficulties between representatives from education and the human services.

Soon it was clear that school personnel had serious complaints about the past performance of those in human services, especially regarding the character of help given to at-risk students. These complaints included the following:

- Delays in responding to referrals from schools.

- Lack of communication back to the schools regarding the status of a case once a referral was made.

- No communication to the schools about the special needs of certain students under agency care when the school did not make the referral (e.g., an adolescent who attempted suicide without the school's knowledge).

- Lack of communication from various community agencies regarding which services are offered, or which services are most appropriate if there is some duplication.

- Lack of a continuing, predictable relationship with agency representatives involved in case management, especially because of high turnover.

- Concern that service personnel in the public and the private sector were fighting among themselves over turf.

- Lack of faith that the long-term needs of students and families referred to agencies were being met.

- A belief that agency personnel lacked the training necessary to educate students in the context of a comprehensive prevention curriculum.

For their part, service agency personnel took umbrage at these criticisms. They cited concerns over confidentiality, large case loads, and limited resources as reasons for poor communication with the schools. Furthermore, agency representatives argued that the school representatives contribute to communication problems in the following ways:

- Students in need are not identified at school and referred to community professionals in a timely manner.

- Schools do not make staff training in identification and referral a priority.

- School services to help students who are at-risk exist on paper, but in fact do not always function as intended. These "paper services" undermine the ability of community organizations to get involved in a timely fashion.

- School personnel who are not properly trained or certified in counseling, are inappropriately taking on clinical responsibilities with students who would best be served by mental health experts.

- Schools do not take advantage of local talent to help in staff training and in curriculum development, even when contacted by agency staff who offer their services.

- Schools do little to develop and implement a curriculum which focuses on the prevention of health risks, including suicide.

This mutual distrust almost destroyed the task force's efforts to develop an effective suicide prevention program. Fortunately, task force leaders sought ways to overcome the mutual distrust that threatened to undermine progress.

Promoting Cooperation

There are several things task force leaders can do to promote cooperation between task force members.

- Acknowledge from the start that people bring to the task force different agendas and experiences, but this is a strength rather than a limitation. Explain that it is an asset to draw upon the diversity of talent and resources available because no single individual or group can solve problems without the help of others.

- Do not refer to past animosity or to failures in collaborative efforts between groups. Emphasize instead examples of successful collaboration in your community and elsewhere.

- Emphasize shared responsibility. It is not uncommon for persons who need help yet who constitute "difficult cases," to be shuffled between organizations. The result is that timely help is not provided and distrust grows between representatives of the organizations. In order to overcome this, establish as a task force priority a "networking" approach to students known to be at high risk of suicide or other dysfunctional behaviors. Included here may be two things: 1) the coordination of programming in school; and 2) the involvement of case managers whose loyalties are not tied to only one organization, but rather to meeting student needs by coordinating the efforts of various groups.

- Establish as a program objective regularly scheduled dialogues between school and agency representatives. Ideally, at least one person should serve as a liaison between schools and agencies. This increases the probabilities of timely information exchange and follow-up.

- Clarify the spheres of competence regarding prevention and intervention efforts. For example, educators are likely to be resentful if agency personnel attempt to direct how and what schools should be teaching students about suicide prevention, or how to run a school peer assistance program. Such programming is within the school's domain of expertise. Similarly, agency staff will resent it if educators, who are not trained in mental health, offer advice on clinical techniques or appropriate therapies for students in treatment.

- Be generous in giving praise and public recognition to all task force members, even if their involvement is minimal. Public recognition tends to create a press for maintaining commitment to task force goals.

- Before any task force directives are issued, solicit feedback from all task force members and any others expected to carry out possible recommendations. By encouraging broad input in the formation of policy, those expected to implement the policy will feel a greater sense of program ownership and a greater willingness to enact the recommendations.

A Word of Caution

The last point listed above bears special emphasis. Although the task force may serve as a *de facto* policy making body, its success rides upon the decentralized operations of constituents throughout the schools and agencies. Any hint of an autocratic approach to policy implementation is likely to alienate those whose support is essential.

The program that emerges should be evaluated for ongoing revisions in light of feedback solicited from those charged with implementation. School and agency administrators should regularly review with subordinates potential changes in task force directives. Persons in leadership positions should avoid voicing criticism as efforts to develop a suicide prevention program get under way. Such criticism will stifle necessary feedback, especially from the line staff whose actions usually determine program success or failure. Again, generous praise can go a long way toward promoting the pride and accountability which guarantee a program's success.

Because knowledge is still emerging, we recognize that there are no pat answers to many vexing questions. We realize that many innovations in the area of youth suicide prevention are experimental and need proper evaluation. Yet we also recognize that many schools and communities have developed unique and effective model prevention programs. The problem of youth suicide is not insurmountable; there are solutions. The bottom line here is obvious: neither schools nor community agencies can be maximally effective if they act alone. By addressing the problem in the context of a public health model, and by fostering in students from very early on the knowledge, skills, and values to make healthy choices, we can and will prevent many young people from taking their own lives.

EPILOGUE

If we are to understand youth suicide, we must look beyond the actions of a distraught individual who, amidst feelings of hopelessness and pain, chooses a path of self-destruction. We must look beyond each adolescent's personal circumstances to the social forces which appear to be placing a generation at risk. We must understand the array of unprecedented and deeply troubling conditions which circumscribe the lives of our young, and which appear to be linked in more than a coincidental fashion to the dramatic rise in the rate of youth suicide.

One thing we believe to be linked to youth suicide is the staggering level of violence in our families. There are nearly three million reported cases of child maltreatment in the United States each year; the number of reports has risen every year since statistics have been available. Many of these children suffer serious long-term psychological impairments, yet receive little or no counseling or other services. Estimates suggest that at least 2 million — perhaps as many as 6 million — women each year are battered by their partners. The American Medical Association estimates that battered women account for 25% of all women who attempt suicide, and 25% of women who seek emergency psychiatric services. When children are living in a home where battering occurs, these children witness the vast majority of violent episodes. The conclusion is obvious: for millions of our young, the home is not a source of warmth and support.

Also affecting the character of family life is the extreme poverty facing nearly one-out-of-four children. Poverty in turn is related to a raft of other problems, including violence in the home and on the streets. Poverty is directly related to the character of community life — or rather the lack of a viable community — in which children are raised. Millions of children live in danger, daily confronting a gauntlet of gangs, drugs, street crime, and dysfunctional adults who are their "neighbors." The climate in which they live is one of threat, uncertainty, and despair. Much of the violence they encounter is public and lethal. Indeed, the sheer level of lethality is exacerbated by easy access to firearms, coupled with a "make my day" ethic which encourages their use. We strongly believe that the lack of a rational gun control policy contributes dramatically to the high number of both youth homicides and suicides.

Problems of community life, especially for those of our young who have been victimized and who are most in need of help, are compounded by another condition: the failings of our *system* of service delivery.

Consider the character of contemporary child protective service agencies. In communities large and small, there have been dramatic increases in the number of referrals to child protective services. Children who are referred need not only protection, but mental health counseling. Yet staff and resources have not grown proportionately. The demand for services is so great that for many, a system of triage exists whereby only the most serious problems are given priority, *if* they come to the attention of authorities. And if they do, there is often little more done than to simply monitor the situation or to provide short term crisis management. Primary prevention and outreach are almost non-existent.

Conditions in the family and the community are related to a host of other problems affecting our young. Substance abuse is rampant among huge numbers of students and their families. Academic failure, social isolation, alienation, sexual exploitation, destructive peer relationships and other problems — all of which are linked to suicide — can also be understood as systemic concerns, and not merely concerns of individuals.

Despite the problems of family and community life which make growing up so difficult for so many of our young, there is cause for hope. Our best hope is through education which teaches all students the knowledge, values and skills necessary to become competent and healthy adults. But with all that is demanded of them, can educators teach such competencies? We believe that they can and must.

It is undeniably true that schools alone cannot necessarily alter the massive problems confronting families and communities. But at the very least, schools can work to minimize the impact of negative social forces on the lives of our young. Schools can do this by seeking to accomplish several broad objectives: providing all students with peer and other support; from an early age teaching students early and consistently appropriate values and competencies; and training all educators to recognize and respond effectively to children in crisis.

We find it a hopeful trend that so many schools are developing intelligent policies and programs to meet these objectives. Peer assistance programs, *required* health and family living courses, staff training in crisis intervention and in prevention programing — the things that were conspicuously absent in schools just a few years ago — are becoming much more common. Fortunately, schools are increasingly including as part of the educational reform movement the need to address social problems.

There seems to be a gradual realization among more and more educators and human service professionals that social problems produce personal problems, and that schools are in a central position to help. There is a realization that for too many students, family and community life fail to meet their basic physical, social, emotional and intellectual needs. Yet there is also the realization that the school constitutes our most hopeful resource; it is a place where our young can acquire the knowledge, skills, support and encouragement to recognize and to avoid exploitation and self-destruction, and ultimately to grow into healthy adults.

APPENDIX A
Postvention Checklist
For Crisis Response Team

❑ Verify the event by contacting the appropriate authorities.

❑ Notify key staff through prearranged telephone chain and schedule staff meeting.

❑ Notify administrators in other buildings who may be affected by the event.

❑ Assemble crisis response team and review facts of the event.

❑ Decide if additional community professionals are needed to help.

❑ Prepare a written memo for teachers to read to their first hour classes.

❑ Prepare a written statement for the media.

❑ Review and modify, if necessary, the first hour procedure for teachers.

❑ Duplicate materials for staff meeting (e.g., written memo, first hour procedure, suicide warning signs, resources, etc.).

❑ Prepare letter to parents informing them of the tragedy and the school's response.

❑ Identify primary survivors within the school (e.g., siblings, cousins, close friends, boyfriend/girlfriend, teammates, teachers), as well as others who might be especially affected (antagonists, persons who may have had foreknowledge of the victim's actions), and monitor their reactions.

❑ Designate referral rooms for individual and small group work.

❑ Assign team members the following responsibilities:

___ designate coordinator to oversee postvention plan;

___ meet with primary survivors;

___ meet with other affected students;

___ assist teachers requesting help during first hour;

___ if necessary, assign substitute teachers to cover classes of teachers most affected by the tragedy;

___ where appropriate, facilitate discussion in each of the victim's classes;

___ assign two team members to visit the deceased's family and provide support and referral where appropriate;

___ designate a media spokesperson;

___ assign a team member to talk to concerned parents.

❑ Develop a confidential list of persons who may need continued follow-up.

❑ Establish student release procedures.

❑ Brief secretaries about how to answer phone calls from parents and the media.

❑ Hold end-of-day staff meetings to debrief and update staff.

❑ Assign at least two members of the team to attend the memorial service and monitor those students present (unless requested by the victim's parents that no one from school attend).

❑ Meet daily for as long as necessary to process referrals and plan follow-up activities.

❑ Arrange for a professional who is not already involved with the crisis team to debrief the team members.

❑ Plan periodic joint meetings with staff and team members to assess all levels of postvention efforts.

❑ Be alert to delayed grief reactions.

APPENDIX B
First Hour Procedure
For Teachers

The implementation of a structured first hour procedure following a traumatic event allows the school to be proactive rather than reactive at the height of a crisis. There are three main goals of this procedure. First, by providing students with factual information and answering their questions, rumors are dispelled. Second, it gives students an opportunity to express intense thoughts and feelings. By normalizing these reactions, anxiety can be decreased and students can begin to regain a sense of control. Finally, a structured procedure provides an opportunity for teachers to identify those students most affected by the event and thereby refer them to the crisis team if appropriate. Below are some of the common elements of a first hour procedure as suggested by a variety of professionals (Barrett, 1987; Patros & Shamoo, 1989; Ruof, Harris & Robbie, 1987; Ryerson & King, 1986).

Read the memo prepared by the administration in a straightforward, calm manner. Announce any changes in school schedule or policy. Let students know that announcements regarding the funeral service will be made as soon as they are available. Students should be discouraged from seeking information by contacting the family of the deceased. If the funeral is held during school hours, inform students that written permission from parents will be required to attend so that they can be excused from classes.

Take a moment to share your own feelings of loss and grief, and acknowledge the great shock and upset everyone is feeling. Anticipate a wide range of emotions and encourage students to share their thoughts and feelings with you and with each other. Take an active role in identifying and reflecting feelings. Allow time for any discussion which students might want to have. If questions come up that you cannot answer, write them down and let students know you will get back to them later. Tell students that if they hear rumors, they should come to *you* rather than their peers. Let them know that rumors only hurt the family and friends of the deceased. Some students will be in shock and may not react at all. Others will begin to cry immediately. Most responses are acceptable and should be encouraged. However, be alert to any behaviors which seem extreme or unusual. In order to encourage students to express their thoughts and feelings, the following questions are helpful:

- "I'm wondering what some of your first *thoughts* are now that you have heard the news. Does anyone else have those thoughts?"

- "I'm wondering what some of your *feelings* are after hearing the news. Does anyone else have those feelings?"

- "When someone dies unexpectedly, it often makes others feel anxious about their own safety or the safety of family and friends. I'm wondering if any of you are worried about someone's safety?"

- "After a sudden death, some people may have trouble sleeping or eating, or may have trouble thinking of anything else. These are normal reactions, but if you are concerned, persons at school are available to help."

- "What is the hardest part of this for you?"

- "Some of you have had people who are close to you die. When you experienced that loss, what kinds of things did you do to take care of yourself? What kinds of things did others say or do that helped you?"

Acknowledge that many students will have strong feelings about the death and may need to leave the classroom to speak to crisis team members. Announce the support services available in the school. Identify the locations of the crisis rooms, and the personnel from school and community agencies who are available for individual or small group support.

Stress that suicide is a choice. Emphasize that everyone has problems, but there are ways to solve problems other than by killing oneself. Acknowledge that it is common for individuals to occasionally think about suicide when things aren't going well, but that thinking about it does not mean acting on it. State that death is final and eliminates all other choices for solving problems. It not only puts an end to who you are in the present, it destroys who you might have been in the future. Re-emphasize that other options are always available when faced with stress and pain, and that talking about feelings with someone who cares is the first step toward making a better choice.

Ask students to support one another. State that if they or any of their friends are preoccupied with thoughts of suicide, they need to talk about it. Tell them that suicide is preventable. They can make a difference in helping to prevent this tragedy from occurring again by getting themselves or their friends adult help if they feel suicidal. Emphasize that IT IS NEVER APPROPRIATE TO KEEP A FRIEND'S SUICIDAL FEELINGS A SECRET. They must act promptly by informing school staff immediately. In addition, encourage students to talk to their parents about their feelings concerning the suicide.

Allow affected students to leave class for counseling services. Some students may need to be escorted to a designated area, perhaps by other students who are more in control. Others will prefer to remain in class. If appropriate, give students passes to be excused from class. Five minutes before the end of the hour, students can either return to the sending teacher and then go back to the crisis room after checking in with the next hour's teacher, OR request that a note from the counselor be sent to the next teacher letting him or her know where the student is. The second option is preferable when the student appears too distraught to leave the crisis room.

Students often benefit from engaging in concrete activities which allow the expression of feelings and which provide an opportunity to say goodbye. Giving students something to do with their feelings and energy is cathartic. Appropriate activities for the class might include the following:

- Composing sympathy cards for the deceased's family and closest friends. These homemade cards could contain expressions of condolences, poetry, or a positive memory of the deceased.

- Writing about favorite memories of the deceased and putting these together in a scrapbook of memories for the family.

- Writing in a journal about their thoughts and feelings after learning about the death.

- Writing about the last time they saw the deceased, and what they wish they could have said if they had known it was the last time they would meet.

- Drawing a picture that represents their thoughts and feelings (for students who prefer drawing to writing).

After sharing feelings and engaging in concrete activities, begin regular classwork when it seems appropriate. However, tests or major reviews should be postponed. Continue with classes the remainder of the day, but allow for additional discussion as the need arises. If discussion continues, ask students to share aloud positive coping strategies they have found helpful when feeling depressed. Any glorification of the suicidal act should be discouraged.

There are several behaviors to watch for which may necessitate immediate referral to the crisis response team. These include the following:

- For those who had a significant emotional relationship with the victim, no reaction to the death.

- Uncontrolled hysteria.

- Extreme disorientation as reflected by repeatedly asking the same questions or displaying a complete lack of responsiveness to the surroundings.

- Physical symptoms of shock, including severe trembling, nausea, dizziness, and difficulty breathing.

- Students whose body language indicates extreme agitation, but who are not talking.

- Verbal or behavioral expressions of extreme anger or a desire for revenge (e.g., swearing, threatening others, slamming or kicking objects, fighting).

- Expressions of intense guilt or anxiety about the death (e.g., blaming self, fearing for own or others' safety).

- Behaviors indicative of suicidal risk.

In addition to the behaviors listed above, there are a number of students at potential risk following a suicide. Be aware of these students and refer those you are concerned about to the crisis response team or other professionals assisting with postvention. Below is a list of students who may be at risk following a suicide:

- relatives and close friends of the victim;

- students involved in a suicide pact with the victim;

- students who were with the victim shortly before or during the suicide;

- students who knew about the suicidal plan but did not act on their knowledge;

- students who had teased, antagonized, or bullied the victim and who may be feeling responsible;

- students with a previous history of suicide attempts;

- students with a recent loss experience who may be reliving "unfinished business" or unresolved conflicts;

- students with a past history of both depression and impulsivity, especially if they live in a dysfunctional home;

- students with weak or nonexistent social support (e.g., transfer students, social isolates);

- students who appear to identify strongly with the victim due to shared interests, social activities, academic performance, or family histories.

If there is a reasonable suspicion that a student displays such characteristics and appears unable to cope with the death, the prudent course of action is to make a referral.

APPENDIX C
First Day Staff Meeting Guidelines

Just as it is important to debrief students most affected by the crisis, so too is it important to debrief staff. Debriefing is best conducted at a staff meeting the end of the first day. Below are some questions designed to help staff members share their thoughts, feelings, and reactions following a traumatic event.

- What went well today and what do you think we could do to improve our handling of the crisis?

- What was it like for you to lead the discussion during the first hour procedure? How did the rest of your classes go?

- What were your thoughts and feelings throughout the day? Did anyone else feel that way? Would anyone like to respond to what _____ just said?

- What are you thinking and feeling as we speak?

- Have any of you had any physical reactions (e.g., nausea, headache, chest pain, dizziness, trembling)?

- What was the most difficult part of the day for you?

- Which students did you feel needed the most help? How did you respond to them?

- What kind of follow-up do you think we need to conduct?

- What suggestions do you have for tomorrow's school day?

- What are you going to do to take care of yourself tonight?

APPENDIX D
Critical Incident Stress Debriefing

Critical Incident Stress Debriefing (CISD)* is intended to mitigate the impact of a traumatic event on those groups exposed to the event. Designed by Jeffrey Mitchell, a specialist in emergency health services, CISD is designed to facilitate the recovery of *normal* people experiencing *normal* symptoms in the context of *abnormal* events. Although originally developed for groups such as paramedics, firefighters, police, and rescue workers following a major crisis or tragedy (e.g., plane crash, hostage situation, bombing), CISD is also appropriate for people in school settings (Mitchell & Everly, 1993).

Since the development of CISD, the technique has been successfully used with both students and school staff following accidental deaths, murders, and suicides. Use of CISD is especially appropriate for those most dramatically affected by trauma because it eases their distress through three interrelated techniques: (1) *ventilation* of thoughts and emotions; (2) *validation* of the normalcy and commonality of certain thoughts and feelings in the aftermath of a crisis; and (3) *education* about stress reactions and ways to cope in the days and weeks following a tragedy.

In schools, CISD groups typically are offered by members of the crisis response team within 24-to-72 hours following a tragedy. Students and school professionals should not be placed in the same group. While most students will have their psychological needs met by school staff during the postvention protocol, those students most

_____

For additional information about CISD, write to: Jeffrey Mitchell, Ph.D., International Critical Stress Foundation, 5018 Dorsey Hall Drive, Suite 104, Ellicott City, MD 21042 deeply affected are candidates for the more intensive and confidential CISD groups.

The CISD groups should be used solely for the purpose of helping people regain a sense of normalcy and control. They are not a substitute for long-term therapy when needed, and they should not be used to critique the job performance or behavior of staff or students. After handling a critical incident for several days, the crisis response team ideally should also undergo debriefing. A professional who is not a member of the crisis response team should conduct this team debriefing.

The process takes members from a cognitive level, to an emotional level, and back to a cognitive level by the end of the group. The process is not necessarily sequential in that group members may jump from thoughts to feelings, back to thoughts, on to behavioral symptoms, and back to feelings again. As long as ventilation, validation, and education take place, however, group members will be helped in the restabilization process. Below is a brief synopsis of the stages that Mitchell has developed for conducting CISD:

I. Introductory Phase

- The group facilitators introduce themselves and express their condolences regarding the event. Members of the group are then asked to introduce themselves.

- Facilitators explain the purpose of the group and the length of time it will meet. Ground rules for the group include the following: (1) a pact of confidentiality — what is said in the room stays in the room (it is acceptable to share one's thoughts and feelings but not what others say and feel); (2)

group members will not be forced to talk and have the option of passing when it is their turn to speak; (3) there will be no "put downs" when others speak — each person should have the opportunity to speak without judgment; (4) people may leave the group session to take care of bodily needs, but are urged to return as soon as possible.

- Facilitators should quell the resistant members by acknowledging that they may not feel the need for debriefing, but their presence and support could help others if they stay.

II. Fact Phase

Facilitators ask participants to describe what they understood to have happened regarding the tragedy. If participants witnessed the tragedy, they should be asked to describe where they were, what they saw and heard, and what they did during and after the event.

III. Thought Phase

- Participants are asked to describe their first *thoughts* as they witnessed the event or when they first learned of the misfortune. They are then asked to share what their thoughts are now.

IV. Emotional Reaction Phase

- Group members are asked to share their emotional reactions to the event as they witnessed it or when they first heard the news. Participants are then asked to share their emotions *now*.

- Facilitators ask participants what has been the worst part of this experience for them.

- Facilitators then normalize people's thoughts and feelings by pointing out common themes.

V. Symptom Phase

- Participants are encouraged to discuss any physiological, behavioral, and emotional symptoms which occurred at the scene and in the days following the incident.

VI. Education Phase

- Facilitators describe immediate and delayed symptoms which are commonly experienced by people in the aftermath of a tragic event.
- Facilitators offer strategies for managing these normal stress related symptoms.
- Facilitators share with participants available community support services and encourage group members to seek additional help if troubling symptoms persist. Because participants may be in a state of shock and confusion following a tragedy, facilitators should provide written handouts on coping strategies and support services to which group members may refer.

VII. Re-entry Phase

- Participants are given an opportunity to ask questions and clarify concerns.

- Facilitators encourage participants to continue offering one another support, and then make themselves available to group members who desire a private meeting.

APPENDIX E
Suicide Prevention Curricula

Below is a selection of highly regarded, commercially available suicide prevention curricula. School personnel should carefully review these curricula before selecting the program which best fits their needs. For schools choosing to develop their own curriculum, we strongly recommend that they select materials which include the major points discussed in *Chapters 11* and *12*.

Suicide Prevention Program for
California Public Schools
School Climate Unit
Instructional Support Services Division
California State Department of Education, 1987
721 Capitol Mall
P. O. Box 944272
Sacramento, CA 94244-2720

The Suicide Prevention Program for California Public Schools is one of the most comprehensive curricula on suicide prevention available. It consists of five lessons designed for grades 9-to-12. An overview of the curriculum is presented, as well as discussion of special concerns in educating students about suicide prevention. Teaching approaches, along with guidelines for grading, are recommended. Each lesson includes a description of goals and objectives, preparation requirements, the complete lesson plan, student handouts and worksheets, and supplementary activities, including guidelines for conducting role plays.

The first lesson begins with an introduction to the problem of youth suicide, including statistics on completions, attempts, and ideation. Ground rules for discussion are established. Students are then asked to take a quiz on suicide myths and facts, followed by a discussion where misperceptions about suicide are dispelled. The students are given an assignment to gather information about community resources for at-risk adolescents and their families. Individual students or teams are assigned an agency and are asked to find out information about the variety and cost of services offered, hours available, if parent permission is necessary, rules on confidentiality, and if the agency can be reached by public transportation. This information becomes part of a community resource list.

Lesson two introduces the topic of depression. This lesson emphasizes that depression often is a common and short-lived reaction to problems we all experience. Students are asked to think back to a time in their life when they felt really "down." They are asked to reflect on how they felt and acted, to whom they talked, and what helped them feel better and get through the difficult time. Students are then taught to recognize warning signs in their friends and classmates. The lesson is concluded with a short vignette involving a dialogue between two students, one of whom might be suicidal. Students are asked to point out warning signs as well as ways to help.

Lesson three reviews various stressors facing students today, and explores the use of alcohol or drugs as a common way many teenagers cope with stress. The link between stress, substance abuse, and suicide is emphasized. A profile of students who are most likely to be at high risk is presented. Positive alternatives to substance use are explored, as are techniques for coping constructively with stress and depression. Finally, guidelines are given on how students can communicate their concern to friends who are abusing alcohol and other drugs.

Lesson four gives students the skills to help friends who are suicidal. The lesson begins with a review of warning signs. Intervention skills are then emphasized, including listening to and reflecting feelings, being honest about and sharing one's own feelings, and getting help from an adult. It is strongly emphasized that keeping a friend's suicidal thinking or plans a secret is dangerous and inappropriate. Students are then given opportunities to practice such skills as initiating discussion with a potentially suicidal friend, making empathic statements, asking directly about suicidal intent, giving support, and lending perspective. Communication stoppers are discussed, including giving unwanted advice, minimizing feelings, making judgmental statements, and trying to solve the friend's problem for them. Finally, a vignette is presented where a student intervenes appropriately with a suicidal friend. The vignette can be read by teachers or students.

The final lesson seeks to increase students' understanding of appropriate resources in the community for themselves and their friends. The lesson begins with a review of the steps in helping a suicidal friend. Students are then taught techniques for encouraging a suicidal friend to seek adult help. Next, students share their reports on community agencies. A master copy of community resources is given to each student. Students are also given information about how to locate help in an emergency.

Suicide Prevention: A Crisis Intervention
Curriculum for Teenagers and Young Adults
By Judie Smith, 1989
Learning Publications, Inc.
P. O. Box 1338
Holmes Beach, Florida 34218-1338

Judie Smith has developed a five lesson suicide prevention unit for adolescents. Each lesson is prefaced with information about its specific goal, planning requirements, time and materials needed, and instructional guidelines for teachers. Student exercises and worksheets are included throughout the curriculum. Smith provides background information to teachers concerning factors contributing to the increase in youth suicide, as well as helpful suggestions for teaching the material.

Lesson one helps students explore their attitudes toward suicide. Teachers are encouraged to be aware of their own attitudes before presenting the exercise to students, and are cautioned to avoid imposing their own beliefs on others. The class is divided into small groups of 5 or 6 students, and each student is presented with a list of open-ended statements regarding suicide (e.g., "I think that suicide is morally _____." "People who attempt suicide are _____."). Each student completes the statements and then is encouraged to share their responses with others in the small group. A group leader is then appointed to summarize the answers to a series of discussion questions (e.g., "Which was the most difficult sentence to complete?"; "What did you learn about your attitudes toward suicide from this exercise?").

The second lesson discusses misconceptions about suicide, and replaces misinformation with facts. A questionnaire with 15 true or false statements is given to each student. Students' responses to the questionnaire are neither collected nor graded. After the class has finished the questionnaire, a discussion of each item follows. Possible homework assignments are suggested, including obtaining local and state statistics on adolescent suicide, researching the legal issues concerning suicide, and presenting a book report on the problem.

Lesson three considers suicide warning signs. Smith suggests first showing a film about teenage suicide to students that emphasizes these warning signs. Questions to guide discussion following the film are provided. Smith cautions teachers to carefully preview films for their content and appropriateness before showing them to students. Following discussion of the film, students are asked to think about a time in their life when everything seemed to go wrong for them and they felt depressed. The teacher then lists three headings on the blackboard: verbal, behavioral, and situational. Students are asked to volunteer information about how they felt, what they did, and what were some of the stressors at the time. Smith emphasizes that no student should be forced to disclose information. Examples are listed under the various headings on the board. Additional warning signs are then added and students receive a handout on warning signs. The lesson ends with a discussion of what students did to cope with the depression. Emphasis is given to the belief that coping and working things out are signs of strength and maturity.

Lesson four teaches effective communication skills. Four exercises are offered which help students to identify and respond to feelings. The first exercise is designed to help students differentiate between thoughts and feelings. During exercises two and three, students are paired up and given a set of statements. One student reads the statement and the other responds by beginning his or her sentence with "You feel _____ because _____. Exercise four is a paper and pencil activity which asks students to choose the most empathic response to a particular statement from a variety of choices. Roadblocks to communication are also discussed, including giving unwanted advice, judging, trying to solve the person's problem for them, interrogating, and analyzing.

The fifth and final lesson emphasizes how to intervene with a suicidal friend. Students are assisted in generating helpful ways to respond to at-risk friends. The teacher writes the suggestions on the blackboard under the headings "What To Do" and "What Not To Do." Students also receive a "Do's and Don'ts" handout. Asking directly about suicidal intent, listening for feelings, offering hope, and getting adult help are emphasized. Vignettes involving potentially suicidal adolescents are provided, and students are asked how they might intervene. The lesson ends with the generation of a list of community resources that provide crisis intervention services to adolescents.

The Gatekeeper Program: A School
Curriculum for Suicide Intervention Skills
Gryphon Place, 1992
1104 S. Westnedge
Kalamazoo, MI 49008

Gryphon Place, a suicide prevention center in Kalamazoo, Michigan, has developed a five lesson unit for high school students. The lessons are prefaced with an explanation of the "gatekeeper" concept. Gatekeepers are defined as those persons who at-risk youth are most likely to turn to during a crisis, and who therefore are in the best position to recognize suicidal risk and get help. The Gatekeeper Program has two goals: (1) to educate student gatekeepers about suicide intervention in hopes of reducing youth suicide; and (2) to assist young people in developing effective coping skills when faced with stress, depression, or problems. An overview of the curriculum is presented, and each lesson includes a description of the goals, behavioral objectives, instructions to the presenter, time requirements, and student handouts or worksheets.

Lesson one begins with a discussion of ground rules. The role of students as "gatekeepers" is explained. Students are then asked to take a 14 item pre-test which measures their knowledge about suicide. Pre-tests are not counted toward a grade, but are used as baseline data to evaluate the impact of the program on students' understanding of suicide prevention and intervention. Next, a film on self-esteem is shown, followed by a discussion of positive and negative coping skills used by students in the film. Students are asked to brainstorm additional positive and negative coping strategies. Lesson one concludes with a discussion on the forces that impact upon one's self-esteem (e.g., parents, friends, media.).

The second lesson begins with the topic of depression. Questions to facilitate discussion are provided to the presenter, as well as points to emphasize during the discussion. These include the common and time-limited nature of depression, that depression results in observable changes in behavior, attitude, and self-image, and that there are always positive coping strategies and resources for dealing with depression. A vignette is presented which illustrates a student experiencing many stressors which begin to erode the capacity to cope constructively. The vignette is designed to help students understand the erosion of coping and problem solving skills that can lead to helplessness, hopelessness, and suicide. Students are then asked to generate healthy ways for the student in the vignette to cope with a "mountain of problems." Presenters are instructed to make a strong link between a negative self-image and feelings of hopelessness and helplessness. Students are asked to make a list of five things they like about themselves as a homework assignment.

In lesson three, students are given a handout on suicide statistics. Instructors use the statistics to demonstrate that although thinking about suicide is quite common, dying from suicide is relatively rare because most people who think about suicide get help. The important role of students as gatekeepers in saving lives is re-emphasized. Next, a handout on suicide facts is disseminated and read aloud. A third handout on warning signs is passed out and read as well. Finally, a selection of readings is used by the instructor to encourage students to listen for problems, feelings, and coping strategies. For homework, students are asked to write down questions they would like to share with the instructor or class.

Lesson four begins with the instructor responding to questions or suggestions made by students as part of their homework assignment from the previous day. Next, communication and intervention skills are reviewed and practiced. Students are asked to complete an exercise where they must correctly identify how another is feeling and then respond empathically. The instructor provides guidance where appropriate. Students are then given a handout which emphasizes intervention skills to be used with a friend in crisis. These include responding empathically, getting adult help, and never promising to keep suicidal intent a secret. Role play scenarios are provided, and 6-8 students are asked to volunteer to demonstrate listening and intervention skills. Observers are then asked to identify the helping techniques demonstrated. The homework assignment asks students to write the name of a responsible adult whom they would go to in a crisis, and to bring that name to class the next day.

The final lesson begins with a review of the key concepts in the curriculum. Students are then asked to verbally identify where they can get adult help for themselves or a friend in crisis. All available school and community resources for students in crisis are shared with the class. Next, students are given additional opportunities to role play appropriate helping skills using the vignettes from lesson four. Finally, the 14 item post-test is administered. In addition, a Likert-type scale is used to rate students' willingness to seek help for their friends or themselves in the event of a suicidal crisis. Students are also asked to assess improvements in their understanding of positive coping strategies as a result of the program.

Suicide: I Don't Want You To Die
By Bill Steele, 1987
New Center CMHS
2051 West Grand Blvd.
Detroit, MI 48208

Bill Steele has designed a video program and a five lesson suicide prevention curriculum for adolescents. The video presents interviews, dramatic scenes, and an unrehearsed group presentation with young people about responding to a suicidal peer. Each of the five lessons includes a description of the objectives, materials, and instructions to the session leaders. Student worksheets are also provided. The workbook for teachers contains an overview of the program, background reading on causal factors implicated in youth suicide, the five lesson curriculum, a crisis intervention protocol to assist suicidal students, a crisis response plan to be used in the aftermath of a suicide, and a program evaluation instrument to assess the impact of the curriculum on students.

The first lesson begins with the teacher presenting statistics and other factual information about suicide. Next, students are given three worksheets aimed at helping them to recognize possible warning signs of suicidal risk. For the first worksheet, students read four short descriptions of at-risk adolescents, and then rate the seriousness of suicidal risk for each individual on a scale from 1 to 10. The second worksheet asks students to review each of the vignettes and make a list of possible clues suggesting suicide potential. The third activity requires students to describe the characteristics and behavior of young people likely to be suicidal. The teacher asks students to generate their lists of warning signs and writes these on the chalkboard. The teacher is instructed to discuss the role of loss experiences in suicidal behavior. The session ends with emphasis by the teacher that warning signs alone cannot determine the level of suicidal risk. Students are asked to come to lesson two prepared to discuss how to know for sure if a peer is suicidal.

In the second lesson, the teacher asks students how they would know if a friend was thinking of suicide. Student responses are listed on the chalkboard. Next, students are asked to review how they rated the students in the vignettes in lesson one for suicidal risk, and to report their ratings with a show of hands. Students are informed that all four vignettes represented young people who actually killed themselves, even though for some of these adolescents there were few warning signs. It is emphasized that one way to know with greater certainty whether a person is suicidal or not is to ask them directly.

The teacher then discusses misconceptions which are detrimental to prevention efforts (e.g., "Asking a friend directly about suicidal intent will give him or her ideas." "People who act suicidal are not serious and only want attention."). Students are then asked how they would respond to someone who admitted they were suicidal. Students are also asked what they would say to a peer who would not admit suicidal intent, but seemed at risk anyway. Teachers guide the discussion so that appropriate responses are reinforced. Suggestions for helping peers are provided (e.g., expressing concern, validating feelings, remaining nonjudgmental, telling suicidal friends that you don't want them to die because you care about them). The session ends with a review of warning signs.

In session three, students are asked to form groups of three or four. Each small group is assigned a series of questions concerning difficult issues not always addressed in suicide prevention programs. Some of these include: (1) how to handle a friend's anger at betraying their "secret"; (2) what to do if an adult does nothing after being told a student is at risk; (3) what to say to a boyfriend or girlfriend who threatens to commit suicide if a break-up occurs; (4) how to respond if a suicidal friend refuses to talk or tries to leave; (5) what to say to a peer who repeatedly gets angry and threatens suicide, but never makes an attempt; and (6) what to say to someone who just got out of the hospital after attempting suicide. Each group elects a spokesperson who reports the responses to the large group. The teacher uses information from the manual to guide discussion of appropriate responses and helpful ways to intervene.

During session four, the 30 minute videotape entitled "I Don't Want You To Die" is shown. Teachers are given discussion guidelines to use following the videotape so that key concepts can be reinforced.

In the fifth and final session, students are given a case study of a student who almost committed suicide. After reading the case study, each student is asked to list the immediate precipitating events that led to suicidal ideation, the long-term circumstances which contributed to suicide vulnerability, and the feelings experienced by the student in the case study as a result of these circumstances. Students are asked to share their lists, followed by group discussion. Teachers are provided with points to emphasize in a discussion guide. The session ends with a reminder to students that other options to suicide are always available, and that there are adults at school who can help. Teachers are encouraged to distribute referral resources if they are available. Students complete the evaluation form before leaving class.

APPENDIX F
Peer Assistant Leadership
Program Resources

National Organizations

National Peer Helpers Association
P.O. Box 2684
Greenville, NC 27858

This association was established in 1987, and serves as a network for peer helping programs around the country. It sponsors a national conference every year, and yearly publishes four issues of the Peer Facilitator Quarterly.

Periodicals

Peer Facilitator Quarterly
P.O. Box 2684
Greenville, NC 27858

Peer Counselor Journal
Editorial Office, Peer Resources
4452 Houlihan Court
Victoria, British Columbia CANADA   V8N 6C6

Program Development

Peer Assistant Leadership Program: Technical Manual
1992
Allegan County Substance Abuse Agency
120 Cutler Street
Allegan, MI 49010
(616) 673-8735

Prevention of Adolescent Problems:
Guidelines for Peer Assistance Program Model
Michigan Dept. of Mental Health Prevention Services,
1989
Lewis Cass Building
Lansing, MI 48913
(517) 335-2361

Peer Helper Training Manual
by J. F. Houghton and A. Lemons, 1985
Department of Defense Dependent Schools
Hoffman Building No. 1
2461 Eisenhower Ave.
Alexandria, VA 22331-1100

High School Peer Resources Programs:
A Director's Perspective
by Ira Sachnoff
69 Sharon Street
San Francisco, CA 94114

Technical Assistance

For technical assistance or consultation in developing a peer helping program, the following persons may be contacted:

Marcia L. McEvoy
Prevention Specialist
Allegan County Community Mental Health Services
P. O. Drawer 130
Allegan, MI 49010
(616) 673-6617

Paul Mailloux, Director
Allegan County Substance Abuse Agency
120 Cutler Street
Allegan, MI 49010
(616) 673-8735

Becky Fatzinger, Prevention Services Supervisor
Van Buren County Community Mental Health Services
P. O. Box 249
Paw Paw, MI 49079-0249
(616) 657-8361

Curricula and Training Materials

**Peervention: Training Peer
Facilitators for Prevention Education**
by Robert Myrick and Betsy Folk
Educational Media Corp.
Box 21311
Minneapolis, MN 55421-0311

**The Power of Peervention:
A Manual for the Training of Peer Facilitators**
by Robert Myrick and Betsy Folk
Educational Media Corp.

Leadership Skills for Peer Group Facilitators
by Joan Sturkie and Charles Hanson
Educational Media Corp.

Conflict Resolution and Mediation for Peer Helpers
by Don Sorenson
Educational Media Corp.

Youth Helping Youth: A Handbook for Training Peer Facilitators (Trainer's Manual – for use with adolescents)
by Robert Myrick and Tom Erney
Educational Media Corp.

Caring and Sharing: Becoming A Peer Facilitator
(Student's Manual - for use with adolescents)
by Robert Myrick and Tom Erney
Educational Media Corp.

Peer Counseling: An In-Depth Look At Training Peer Helpers (Trainer's Manual)
by Judith Tindall and H. Dean Gray
Accelerated Development
3400 Kilgore Ave.
Muncie, IN 47304-4896

Peer Power: Becoming An Effective Peer Helper, Book 1, Introductory Program (Student's Manual)
by Judith Tindall and H. Dean Gray
Accelerated Development

Peer Power: Book 2, Applying Peer Helping Skills
(Student's Manual)
by Judith Tindall
Accelerated Development

Children Helping Children: Teaching Students to Become Friendly Helpers (Trainer's Manual – for use with elementary or junior high school students)
by Robert Myrick and Robert Bowman
Educational Media Corp.

Becoming A Friendly Helper: A Handbook for Student Facilitators (Student's Manual - for use with elementary or junior high school students)
by Robert Myrick and Robert Bowman
Educational Media Corp.

Friends Helping Friends: A Manual for Peer Counselors (Student's Manual)
by Carol Painter
Educational Media Corp.

Tutoring: Learning by Helping (Student handbook for training peer and cross-age tutors)
by Elizabeth Sabrinsky Foster
Educational Media Corp.

Curriculum Guide for Student Peer Counseling Training (Trainer's Guide)
by Barbara Varenhorst
Educational Media Corp.

Natural Helpers: A Peer Support Program – Naturally, A Leader's Guide
by Jane Akita and Carol Mooney
Comprehensive Health Education Foundation
20814 Pacific Highway South
Seattle, Washington 98188

The Peer Counseling Starter Kit
by Rey Carr and Greg Saunders
Peer Resources Bookstore
4452 Houlihan Court
Victoria, British Columbia   V8N 6C6

Peer Counselor's Workbook (Student's Guide to
accompany Starter Kit)
by Gail Roberts
Peer Resources Bookstore

Kids Helping Kids
(Manual for training elementary peer helpers)
by Trevor Cole
Peer Resources Bookstore

Peer Helping: Indexed and Annotated Bibliography,
updated to 1993.
Peer Resources Bookstore

**Peer Teaching and Tutoring: An Indexed
And Annotated Bibliography,** updated to 1993.
Peer Resources Bookstore

**Peer Helping Implementation,
Maintenance, and Research Issues**
by David de Rosenroll
Peer Resources Bookstore

REFERENCES

Akita, J., & C. Mooney. (1982). *Natural helpers: A peer support program — naturally.* Seattle, WA: Comprehensive Health Education Foundation.

American Association of Suicidology. (1991). *Postvention guidelines.* School Suicide Prevention Programs Committee. Denver, CO.

Barrett, T. (1985). Does suicide prevention in the schools have to be a 'terrifying' concept? *Newslink, 11* (1), 3.

Barrett, T. (1987). *Youth in crisis: Seeking solutions to self- destructive behavior.* Longmont, CO: Sopris West.

Berman, A. (1987). Suicide prevention: A critical need and a critical prespective. *In A. McEvoy (Chair), Presented at the* National Conference on Suicide Prevention and the Schools. Orlando, FL.

Berman, A. (1991). Suicide intervention in schools: Critical reflections. In A. Leenaars & S. Wenkstern (Eds.), *Suicide prevention in schools.* NY: Hemisphere Publishing Corp.

Berman, A., & D. Jobes. (1991). *Adolescent suicide, assessment, and intervention.* Washington, DC: American Psychological Association.

Blyth, D., Simmons, R., & S. Carlton-Ford. (1983). The adjustment of early adolescents to school transitions. *Journal of Early Adolescence, 3,* 105-120.

Boggs, M. (1987). *Suicide prevention in educational settings.* Unpublished manuscript, Suicide Prevention Center, Dayton, OH.

Botvin, G., Baker, E., Renick, N. Filazzola, A., & E. Botvin. (1984). A cognitive-behavioral approach to substance abuse prevention. *Addictive Behavior, 9,* 137-147.

Bowman, R. (1982). *A student facilitator program: Fifth graders helping primary grade problem-behavior students.* Unpublished doctoral dissertation, University of Florida, Gainsville, FL.

Bowman, R. & R. Myrick. (1987). Effects of an elementary school peer facilitator program on children with behavior problems. *The School Counselor, 34,* 369-378.

Bowman, R., & R. Myrick. (1980). I'm a junior counselor having lots of fun. *School Counselor, 28,* 31-38.

Brent, D., Pepper, J., Moritz, G., Baugher, M., Roth, C., Balach, L., & J. Schweers. (1993). Stressful life events, psychopathology, and adolescent suicide: A case control study. *Suicide and Life-threatening Behavior, 23,* 179-187.

Callahan, J. (1988). *Guidelines for school-based survivors of suicide support groups.* Unpublished paper. University of Michigan, Ann Arbor, MI.

Callahan, J. (1989). *Negative effects of school postvention programs.* Paper presented at the annual meeting of the American Association of Suicidology, San Diego.

California State Department of Education. (1987a). *Suicide prevention program for California public schools.* Sacramento, CA:

California State Department of Education (1987b). *Youth suicide prevention school program: Final evaluation report.* Sacramento, CA.

Caplan, G. (1964). *Principles of preventive psychiatry.* New York: Basic Books.

Capuzzi, D. (1989). *Adolescent suicide prevention: Counseling and intervention strategies* (2nd ed.). Ann Arbor, MI: ERIC Counseling and Personnel Services Clearinghouse.

Centers for Disease Control. (1988). CDC recommendations for a community plan for the prevention and containment of suicide clusters. *Morbidity and Mortality Weekly Report, 37* (Supp. S-6), Atlanta, GA.

Coleman, L. (1987). *Suicide clusters.* Boston: Faber & Faber.

Comstock, B., Simmons, J., and J. Franklin. (1989). Community response to adolescent suicide clusters. In M. Feinleib, (Ed.), *Report of the secretary's task force on youth suicide: Prevention and intervention in youth suicide, 3,* (pp 72-79). Washington, DC: U.S. DHHS Publication No. ADM 89-1623. U.S. Government Printing Office.

Davis J., & J. Sandoval. (1991). *Suicidal youth: School-based intervention and prevention.* San Francisco: Jossey-Bass.

Dunne, E., McIntosh, J., & K. Dunne-Maxim. (1987). *Suicide and its aftermath: Understanding and counseling the survivors.* New York: W.W. Norton & Co.

Fairfax County Public Schools. (1987). *Adolescent suicide prevention program: A guide for schools and communities.* Faixfax, VA.

Felner, R. (1990). Asking 'good' questions in prevention research. *Newslink, 16,* (2), 16-17.

Felner, R., & A. Adan. (1988). The school transition environment project: An ecological intervention and evaluation. In R. Price, E. Cowen, R. Lorian, & J. Ramos-McKay (Eds.), *14 Ounces of prevention: A casebook for practitioners.* Washington, DC: American Psychological Association.

Felner, R., Ginter, M., & J. Primavera. (1982). Primary prevention during school transitions: Social support and environmental structure. *American Journal of Community Psychology, 10,* 277-290.

Felner, R., Primavera, J., & A. Cauce. (1981). The impact of school transition: A focus for preventive efforts. *American Journal of Community Psychology, 9,* 449-459.

Foster, E. (1993). *Tutoring: Learning by helping.* Minneapolis: Educational Media Corp.

Gallup Organization, Inc. (1991). *Teenage suicide study: Executive summary.* Princeton, NJ.

Garbarino, J., Guttman, E., & J. Seely. (1986). *The psychologically battered child: Strategies for identification, assessment, and intervention.* San Francisco: Jossey-Bass.

Garbarino, J., Dubrow, N., Kostelny, K., & C. Pardo. (1992). *Children in danger: Coping with the consequences of community violence.* San Francisco: Jossey-Bass.

Garrison, C., Lewinson, P., Marsteller, F., Langhinrichsen, J. & I. Lann. (1991). The assessment of suicidal behavior in adolescents. *Suicide and Life-threatening Behavior, 21,* 217-230.

Getz, W., Allen, B., Myers, R., & K. Linder. (1983). *Brief counseling with suicidal persons.* Lexington, MA: Lexington Books/D.C. Health.

Gilchrist, L., Schinke, S., Snow, R., Schilling, R., & V. Senechal. (1988). The transition to junior high school: Opportunities for primary prevention. *Journal of Primary Prevention, 8,* 99-108.

Gryphon Place (1992). *Gatekeeper suicide prevention school curriculum evaluations.* Unpublished data. Gryphon Place: Kalamazoo, MI.

Hafen, A., & K. Frandsen. (1986). *Youth suicide: Depression and loneliness.* Evergreen, CO: Cordillera Press.

Hirsch, B., & B. Rapkin. (1987). The transition to junior high school: A longitudinal study of self-esteem, psychological symptomatology, school life, and social support. *Child Development, 58,* 1235-1243.

Hoover, T. (1984). Peer culture development: A focus on the behavioral problem student. *Small Group Behavior, 15,* 511- 525.

Houghton, J., & A. Lemons. (1985). *Peer helper training manual.* Department of Defense Dependent Schools, Alexandria, VA.

Huey, W. (1985). Informational-processing groups: A peer led orientation approach. *The School Counselor, 33,* 3-8.

James, J., & F. Cherry. (1988). *The grief recovery handbook: A step-by-step program for moving beyond loss.* New York: Harper and Row.

Johnson, C. (1978). Improving learning through peer leadership. *Phi Delta Kappan, 59,* (8), 560.

Johnson, S., & L. Maile. (1987). *Suicide and the schools: A handbook for prevention, intervention, and rehabilitation.* Springfield, IL: C. C. Thomas.

Kalafat, J. & M. Elias. (1991). Evaluation of school-based interventions. In A. Leenaars and S. Wenkstern (Eds.), *Suicide prevention in schools.* NY: Hemisphere Publishing Corp.

Kalafat, J. & D. Ryerson. (1989). A review of evaluation procedures and priorities. *Newslink, 15,* (3), 1-6.

Kelson vs. The City of Springfield, Oregon. (1985). 767 F. 2d 651: Ninth Circuit Court of Appeals.

Klott, J. (1988a). *Suicide assessment and intervention.* Workshop presented to the Responding to Adolescent Problems Task Force, Allegan, MI.

Klott, J. (1988b). *Gryphon Place suicide survivor manual.* Kalamazoo, MI: Gryphon Place.

Lamb, F., & K. Dunne-Maxim. (1987). Postvention in schools: Policy and process. In E. Dunne, J. McIntosh, & K. Dunne-Maxim (Eds.), *Suicide and its aftermath: Understanding and counseling the survivors.* (pp. 245-263). New York: Norton.

Lavin, A., Shapiro, G., & K. Weill. (1992). *Creating an agenda for school-based health promotion: A review of selected reports.* Boston: Harvard School of Public Health.

Lester, D. (1991). *Psychotherapy for suicidal clients.* Springfield, IL: Charles C. Thomas.

Luepker, R., Johnson, C., & P. Murphy. (1983). Prevention of cigarette smoking: Three year follow-up of an educational program for youth. *Journal of Behavioral Medicine, 6,* 53- 62.

Maher, C., & R. Christopher. (1982). Preventing high school maladjustment: Effectiveness of professional and cross-age behavioral group counseling. *Behavior Therapy, 13,* 259-270.

Maris, R., Berman, A., Maltsberger, J., & R. Yufit, (Eds.), (1992). *Assessment and prediction of suicide.* NY: Guliford.

McEvoy, M., & LeClaire, D. (1993). *The PAL (Peer Assistant Leadership) program: A comprehensive model for suicide prevention.* Workshop presented at the Conference of the National Organization of Student Assistance Programs and Partners, Chicago, IL.

McEvoy, A., & M. McEvoy. (1992). Understanding: When students commit suicide. *School Intervention Report, 6,* (2), 1-19.

McEvoy, M., & A. McEvoy. (1991). Creating peer assistance programs. *School Intervention Report, 5,* (5), 1-22.

McEvoy, M., & A. McEvoy. (1990). Reducing suicide contagion. *School Intervention Report, 4,* (3), 1-16.

Michigan Department of Mental Health Prevention Services. (1989). *Prevention of adolescent problems: Guidelines for peer assistance program model.* Lansing, MI.

Michigan Model State Steering Committee. (1991). *Michigan Model for Comprehensive School Health Education Implementation Plan.* Lansing, MI.

McIntosh, J. (1993). Primary prevention: What can AAS do? *Newslink, 19,* (2), 3.

Miller, M. (1984). *Training workshop manual.* San Diego, CA: Suicide Information Center.

Mitchell, J., & G. Everly. (1993). *Critical incident stress debriefing (CISD): An operations manual for the prevention of traumatic stress among emergency services and disaster workers.* Ellicott City, MD: Chevron Corp.

Mitchell, W., McGee, S., & L. Tompkins. (1985). *Training and using peer facilitators for orientation of students in secondary schools.* New Orleans, LA: National Association of Social Workers, Report No. CG-018-250.

Motto, J. (1978). Recognition, evaluation and management of persons at risk for suicide. *Personnel and Guidance Journal,* 537-543.

Murphy, F. (1975). *A study of the effects of peer group counseling on attendance at the senior high level.* Unpublished doctoral dissertation. George Washington University.

Myrick, R., & R. Bowman. (1981a). *Children helping children: Teaching students to become friendly helpers.* Minneapolis: Educational Media Corp.

Myrick, R., & R. Bowman. (1981b). *Becoming a friendly helper: A handbook for student facilitators.* Minneapolis: Educational Media Corp.

Myrick, R., & T. Erney. (1985). *Youth helping youth: A handbook for training peer facilitators.* Minneapolis: Educational Media Corp.

Myrick, R., & T. Erney. (1984). *Caring and sharing: Becoming a peer facilitator.* Minneapolis: Educational Media Corp.

New Jersey State Department of Human Services, Division of Mental Health and Hospitals. (1989). *Youth suicide prevention: Meeting the challenge in New Jersey schools.* Trenton, NJ.

Orbach, I., & H. Bar-Joseph. (1993). The impact of a suicide prevention program for adolescents on suicide tendencies, hopelessness, ego identity, and coping. *Suicide and Life-Threatening Behavior, 23,* 120-129.

Patros, P., & Shamoo, T. (1989). *Depression and suicide in children and adolescents: Prevention, intervention, and postvention.* Boston: Allyn & Bacon, Inc.

Pfeffer, C. (1986). *The suicidal child.* NY: Guilford Press.

Poland, S. (1989). *Suicide intervention in the schools.* New York: Guilford Press.

Poland, S., & G. Pitcher. (1990). Best practices in crisis intervention. In A. Thomas & J. Grimes (Eds.), *Best practices in school psychology - II.* (pp. 259-274). Washington, DC: National Association of School Psychologists.

Ross, C. (1985). Teaching children the facts of life and death: Suicide prevention in the schools. In M. Peck, N. Farberow, & R. Litman (Eds.), *Youth suicide.* (pp. 147-169). NY: Springer Publishing Co.

Rotheram, M. (1987). Evaluation of imminent danger for suicide among youth. *American Journal of Orthopsychiatry, 57,* 102- 110.

Rouf, S., & J. Harris. (1988a). How to get suicide prevention training and a crisis team for your schools. *Communique, 16,* (10), 28.

Rouf, S., & J. Harris. (1988b). How to select, train, and supervise a crisis team. *Communique, 16,* (12), 19.

Rouf, S., & J. Harris. (1988c). Q and A on legal issues related to suicide. *Communique, 16,* (6), 18.

Ruof, S., Harris, J., & M. Robbie. (1987). *Handbook: Suicide prevention in the schools.* La Salle, CO: Weld Boces.

Ryerson, D. (1987a). ASAP - An adolescent suicide awareness programme. In R. Diekstra & K. Hawton (Eds.), *Suicide in adolescence.* Dordrecht, Netherlands: Martinus Nijhoff.

Ryerson, D. (1987b). *Schools and community based organizations working toward suicide prevention.* In A. McEvoy (Chair), Presented at the National Conference on Suicide Prevention and the Schools. Orlando, FL.

Ryerson, D., & B. King. (1986). *Adolescent suicide awareness program: A comprehensive education and prevention program for school communities.* Lyndhurst, NJ: South Bergan Mental Health Center.

Samuels, D., & M. Samuels. (1975). *The complete handbook of peer counseling.* Miami, FL: Fiesta Publishing.

Shaffer, D., Vieland, V., Garland, A., Rojas, M., Underwood, M., & C. Busner. (1990). Adolescent suicide attempters: Response to suicide-prevention programs. *Journal of the American Medical Association, 264,* 3151-3155.

Shope, J., Marcoux, B., & J. Thompson. (1989). *School-based adolescent substance abuse prevention,* Unpublished Manuscript, University of Michigan School of Public Health, Ann Arbor, MI.

Simmons, R., Burgeson, R., Carlton-Ford, S., & D. Blyth. (1987). The impact of cumulative change in early adolescence. *Child Development, 58,* 1220-1234.

Smith, K. (1988). *Psychotherapy of the suicidal patient.* A paper presented at the second annual conference of the Michigan Association of Suicidology, Lansing, MI.

Smith, K., Eyeman, J., Dyck, R., & D. Ryerson. (1988). *Report of the school suicide programs questionnaire.* Denver: American Association of Suicidology.

Steele, B. (1992). *Preventing self destruction: A manual for school crisis response teams.* Holmes Beach, FL: Learning Publications.

Telch, M., Kellen, J., & A. McAllister. (1982). Long-term follow-up of pilot project on smoking prevention with adolescents. *Journal of Behavioral Medicine, 5,* 1-8.

Tierney, R., Ramsay, R., Tanney, B., & W. Lang. (1991). Comprehensive school suicide prevention programs. In A. Leenaars & S. Wenckstern. (Eds.), *Suicide prevention in schools* (pp. 83-98). NY: Hemisphere Publishing Corp.

Tierney, R., & W. Lang. (1991). Cutting suicide prevention programs in schools. *Newslink, 17,* (2), 8-9.

Tindall, J. (1979). *Youth listener evaluation survey.* St. Louis: Lafayette High School.

Tindall, J., & H. Gray. (1988). *Peer power: Becoming an effective peer helper, Book 1 introductory program.* Muncie, IN: Accelerated Development, Inc.

Tindall, J. (1989). *Peer power: Book 2, Applying peer helper skills.* Muncie, IN: Accelerated Development, Inc.

Tindall, J., & H. Gray. (1989). *Peer counseling: An in-depth look at training peer helpers.* Muncie, IN: Accelerated Development, Inc.

Tobler, N. (1986). Meta-analysis of 143 adolescent drug prevention programs: Quantitative outcome results of program participants compared to a control or comparison group. *Journal of Drug Issues, 16,* 537-567.

U.S. Department of Health and Human Services. (1989). *Report of the secretary's task force on youth suicide.* (DHHS Publication No. ADM 89-1621-1624). 1-4. Washington, DC: Government Printing Office.

Varenhorst, B. (1980). *Curriculum guide for student peer counseling training.* Minneapolis, MN: Educational Media Corp.

Vega, W., Gil, A., Warheit, G., Apospori, E., & R. Zimmerman. (1993). The relationship of drug use to suicide ideation and attempts among African American, Hispanic, and White Non-Hispanic male adolescents. *Suicide and Life-Threatening Behavior, 23,* (2), 110-119.

Wenkstern, S., & A. Leenars. (1991). "Suicide postvention: A case illustration in a secondary school." In A. Leenars & S. Wenkstern (Eds.), *Suicide prevention in schools.* (pp 181- 195). NY: Hemisphere Publishing Corp.

Yufit, R. (1991). American Association of Suicidology Presidential Address: Suicide assessment in the 1990's. *Suicide & Life-Threatening Behavior, 21,* (2), 152-163.

Yufit, R. (1989). Assessment of suicide potential. In R.J. Craig (Ed.), *Clinical and Diagnostic Interviewing* (pp. 289-304). Northvale, NJ: Jason Aronson.

ADDITIONAL
SUGGESTED READINGS

Beck, A., Steer, R., Beck, J., & C. Newman. (1993). Hopelessness, depression, suicide ideation, and clinical diagnosis of depression. *Suicide and Life-Threatening Behavior, 23,* 139-145.

Berman, A. (1990). *Suicide prevention: Case consultations.* NY: Springer.

Blumenthal, S., & D. Kupfer. (Eds.), (1990). *Suicide over the life cycle: Risk factors, assessment, and treatment of suicidal patients.* Washington, DC: American Psychiatric Press.

Bolton, I. (1983). *My son . . . my son . . .: A guide to healing after a suicide in the family.* Atlanta: Bolton Press.

Bongar, B. (Ed.), (1992). *Suicide: Guidelines for assessment, management and treatment.* NY: Oxford University Press.

Bongar, B. (1992). *The suicidal patient: Clinical and legal standards.* Washington, DC: American Psychological Association.

Brent, D., Perper, J., Allman, C., Moritz, G., Wartella, M., & J. Zelenak. (1991). The presence and accessibility of firearms in the homes of adolescent suicides. *Journal of the American Medical Association, 266,* 2989-2995.

Chance, S. (1992). *Stronger than death.* NY: W.W. Norton.

De La Rosa, M., & J. Recio, (Eds.), (1993). *Drug abuse among minority youth: Advances in research and methodology.* Rockville, MD: National Institute of Drug Abuse.

Diekstra, R., Maris, R., Platt, S., & G. Sonnek, (Eds.), (1989). *Suicide and its prevention: The role of attitude and imitation.* Leiden, Netherlands: Published under the auspices of the World Health Organization, E.J. Brill.

Evans, G., & N. Farberow. (1988). *The encyclopedia of suicide.* NY: Facts on File.

Feindler, E., & G. Kalfus. (1990). *Adolescent behavior therapy handbook.* NY: Springer Publishing Co.

Grossman, D. Soderberg, R., & F. Rivara. (1993). Prior injury and motor vehicle crash as risk factors for youth suicide. *Epidemiology, 4,* 115-119.

Hazell, P., & T. Lewin. (1993). Friends of adolescent suicide attempters and completers. *Journal of the American Academy of Child and Adolescent Psychiatry, 32,* 76-81.

Jacobs, D. (1992). *Suicide and clinical practice.* Washington, DC: American Psychiatric Press.

Kirk, W. (1993). *Adolesecnt suicide: A school-based approach to assessment and intervention.* Champaign, IL: Research Press.

Leenaars, A. (1993). Suicide and gun control. *Newslink, 19,* (2), 9.

Lester, D. (1992). *Why people kill themselves: A 1990s summary of research findings on suicidal behavior.* Springfield, IL: Charles C. Thomas.

Lester, D. (1992) *Suicide behind bars: Prediction and prevention.*. Philadelphia: Charles Press.

McEvoy, A. (1992). *When disaster strikes: Preparing schools for bus accidents, murders, suicides, tornados and other community catastrophes.* Holmes Beach, FL: Learning Publications.

McEvoy, A., & E. L. Erickson. (1994). *Abused children: The educator's guide to primary prevention and intervention.* Holmes Beach, FL: Learning Publications, Inc.

McIntosh, J. (1993). Control group studies of suicide survivors: A review and critique. *Suicide and Life-Threatening Behavior, 23,* 146-161.

Murphy, G.E. (1992). *Suicide in Alcoholism.* NY: Oxford University Press.

Richman, J. (1986). *Family therapy for suicidal people.* NY: Springer.

Shneidman, E. (1985). *Definition of suicide.* NY: Wiley.

Smith, J. (1992). *Drugs and suicide.* Rosen Group.

Shamoo, T. (1992). *Helping your child cope with depression and suicidal thoughts.* NY: Free Press.

Swanson, J., Linskey, A., Quintero-Salinas, R., Pumariega, A., & C. Holzer. (1992). A binational school survey of depressive symptoms, drug use, and suicidal ideation.

Journal of the American Academy of Child and Adolescent Psychiatry, 31, 669–678.

Wallace, H., Patrick, K., Parcel, G., & J. Igoe, (Eds.). (1992). *Principles and practices of student health.* Vol. 1-3. Oakland, CA: Third Party Publishing Co.

Whitaker, L., & R. Slimak, (Eds.). (1990). *College student suicide.* NY: The Haworth Press.

NOTES

NOTES